The Origin and Early Form of Greek Tragedy

THE ORIGIN AND
EARLY FORM OF
GREEK TRAGEDY

Gerald F. Else

The Norton Library
W · W · NORTON & COMPANY · INC ·
NEW YORK

Books That Live
The Norton imprint on a book means that in the publisher's
estimation it is a book not for a single season but for the years.
W. W. Norton & Company, Inc.

Library of Congress Cataloging in Publication Data

Else, Gerald Frank, 1908–
    The origin and early form of Greek tragedy.

    Original ed. issued as v. 20 of Martin classical
lectures.
    Includes bibliographical references.
    1.   Greek drama (Tragedy)—History and criticism.
I.   Title.   II.   Series: Martin classical lectures,
v. 20.
[PA6068.E4   1972]   882'.051   72-7047
ISBN 0-393-00656-5

PRINTED IN THE UNITED STATES OF AMERICA

2 3 4 5 6 7 8 9 0

In Memory of
Martha

Foreword

The solution proposed in these pages for the problem of the origin of tragedy is a radical one, or will seem so to many readers; though from another point of view it might be called conservative. It involves rejecting certain crucial pieces of evidence which are usually regarded as the foundation of all we know about the subject. But how can one hope to achieve a viable theory of the origin of tragedy if one begins by rejecting the guidance not only of the *Poetics* but of anthropology and religion: in short, by turning one's back on Dionysus?

I will confess that doubts about the soundness of my procedure have assailed me at various times, both before the lectures were given and since. But repeated consideration of the problem has convinced me that the doubts were not really about the procedure; they were prompted by the radical divergence between my *results* and those reached by others, including some of the soundest and most respected scholars who have dealt with the matter. The final upshot is that I hold to the views put forward in the lectures. It seems to me that a consistent spirit and a consistent logic were at work in the creation of tragedy by Thespis and Aeschylus, whereas if one begins with Dionysus—with or without satyrs—one is committed to an alleged "development" which is illogical, even anti-logical. And one is committed to it without necessity; for the evidence which is commonly supposed to make it necessary, that of the *Poetics,* is itself the product of a theory. Indeed it cannot be said too early or too often that anyone who deals with the origin of tragedy is theorizing.

Aristotle theorized, and so must we; he had too few facts to do otherwise, and so have we.

Thus the substance of my four lectures appears here essentially unaltered. But in preparing them for publication I found myself confronted with serious problems of length and documentation. It is all very well, for example, in an hour's lecture, to sketch out the most important existing theories and suggest their weaknesses. But sketches and suggestions are not enough in a book which is submitted to the judgment of the scholarly world, especially if it challenges a widely held consensus. Hence the first chapter in particular has been considerably reworked and expanded, to cover the main theories more fully and show their bases and their implications. On the other hand, the coverage could not have been made really complete, and the intricate web of argument concerning our sources or alleged sources could not have been spread before the reader in full, without developing the chapter into a book of its own and so overbalancing the rest of the discussion. For better or worse the chapter takes a middle way; I can only hope it is a tolerable compromise within the framework of my purpose.

In spite of the reworking, then, the book does not attempt to give an exhaustive treatment of every aspect of the whole subject, and the documentation, especially outside the first chapter, is correspondingly sparse. In the last chapter, for example, very little of the extensive literature on Aeschylus is cited. If my over-all point of view commends itself to other scholars, much more detailed work will need to be done on his dramaturgy.

There remains the pleasant task of thanking the Martin Lecture Committee, whose invitation gave me the opportunity to expound these unorthodox ideas, and especially its secretary, my old friend Charles Murphy. A special debt of gratitude must be recorded to Professor Alfred C. Schlesinger of Oberlin, himself the author of a valuable book on tragedy in this same series, and to two unnamed readers for the Harvard University Press, all of whom read my text with care and made trenchant criticisms and many helpful suggestions. Finally, Miss Virginia Wharton and the Editorial Department of the Harvard University Press have given the book their customary exact attention and earned my best thanks.

The Martin Lectures have a proud tradition of humanistic scholarship in the classical field. I hope sincerely that these chapters are not unworthy of that tradition.

Gerald F. Else

Ann Arbor, Michigan
1 March 1965

Contents

Introduction

THE READER is entitled to know at the outset what to expect from still another treatment of the origin of tragedy. Is it going to thresh the same old straw once more, or has it significantly new evidence to present? There is no simple answer to this apparently straightforward question. On the one hand I have no new evidence to offer, if by "evidence" one means explicit statements from antiquity about the origin of tragedy. The few available rags and tatters of that sort are already known to everybody; they have been discussed endlessly and used to support very different kinds of theory. On the other hand there is a considerable range of evidence which either has not been adduced at all, because it was not thought to have any bearing on the subject, or has been misapplied because certain preconceptions prevented it from being viewed in the right light.

This other body of evidence, in spite of its variousness, has one common trait: it all pertains to Athens. This book is concentrated on the Athenian development, for the simple reason that—in my opinion—there was no other. Whatever may have happened elsewhere in Greece, whatever analogues (none of them true ones, for that matter) may appear in Egypt, Mexico, or Polynesia, tragedy has never come to birth anywhere in the world except in Athens in the sixth century B.C. Frustrating though it is to have so little solid evidence from that period, we are condemned to work with what we do have and make what we can of it. And actually, if one looks at the matter from a larger point of view, the evidence is not quite so sparse after all. If we put together what we know or can confidently postulate about Solon, Pisistratus, Thespis, Aeschylus, and the tragic contests in the fifth century, a single and consistent line of development emerges, beginning with Thespis.

Yet "development" is not the right word. The essential novelty of my approach to the subject is the belief that tragedy was not the end-result of a gradual development but the product of two successive *creative acts* by two men of genius. The first of these men was Thespis, the second was Aeschylus. If Thespis did not exist, that is, if we had no tradition concerning him, it would be necessary to invent him. Fortunately Aeschylus exists beyond any doubt, and enough of his work is available so that we can define its point and bearing for our purpose—especially now that the redating of his *Suppliants*[1] has cleared the way for a new appraisal. What emerges is not so much a development as a field of force in which two crucial acts can be identified: the creation of *tragôidia* by Thespis, the creation of tragic drama by Aeschylus.

This view of the matter differs in important ways from Aristotle's, and from any view based on his testimony or apparent testimony in the *Poetics;* for Aristotle is the classic apostle of development (*pollas metabolas metabalousa,* "having gone through many changes," *Poetics* 4. 1449a14). But it also differs from many other theories which ignore or even contradict Aristotle. The common element in these theories, indeed in almost all modern reconstructions, is that they trace the origin of tragedy to one or more *pre-existing sources*: dithyramb, *satyrikon,* vegetation rituals, initiation rites, hero-cult, lamentations for the dead, etc. The role of Thespis is, then, to have modified or adapted the pre-existing form by introducing what is conventionally called the "first actor," and this is thought of either as adding a new dimension to what had been a strictly choral performance or as bringing out in sharper relief a dimension which was already implicit in it: that of "dialogue" or "drama." In any case—and this again is characteristic of practically all theories of the origin of tragedy, ancient or modern, whether based on the *Poetics* or not—the pre-existing source is assumed to be a choral or at least some kind of a group performance. This group activity is successively modified by the introduction of an individual (by Thespis) and then of another and another (Aeschylus, Sophocles), until finally the individuals, that is, the actors, begin to predominate over the group (Aeschylus) and in their action and interaction with each other tragedy attains its perfect form (Sophocles).

The sequence I have just sketched seems at first blush to provide a plausible and consistent development, from the first germs of drama to its final unfolding. Why, then, is there no agreement on its exact starting point or its course? For in spite of what was said above about common elements and assumptions, hardly any two modern theories agree on any particular point in the development. I emphasize this here, at the beginning of our discussion, because among the general literate public, and even among many classical scholars who have not labored in this part of the vineyard, there is a widespread impression that a general consensus exists. "Everybody knows" that tragedy came out of the dithyramb, or the satyr-drama, or both, or—this particularly in English-speaking countries—that its source was a certain primitive ritual sequence first described by Gilbert Murray. Thus Francis Fergusson in *The Idea of a Theatre,* one of the most penetrating and influential books written on the drama in our time, states as a fact: "The Cambridge School of Classical Anthropologists has shown in great detail that the form of Greek tragedy follows the form of a very ancient ritual, that of the *Eniautos-Daimon,* or seasonal god."[2]

The real fact is that Gilbert Murray never demonstrated either the existence of such a ritual sequence in preclassical Greece or its survival in the extant tragedies. This was shown in detail by Pickard-Cambridge over thirty years ago,[3] and the theory is not now held, at least in its strict form, by any leading scholar.[4] But this state of affairs appears to have been unknown to Fergusson, and is certainly unknown to many others.

Such manifestations of intellectual lag between one field and another, though perhaps inevitable in our overspecialized world, are discouraging when their effect is to impede understanding not only of the origin of tragedy but of the extant plays themselves. The notion that Sophocles' audience approached his tragedies in a spirit of "ritual expectancy" does serious damage to our interpretation of the plays, and through them to our conception of tragedy as a whole.[5]

Murray's alleged ritual sequence and the misreadings and misinterpretations that have flowed from it are a particular instance of a much broader, more pervasive phenomenon: the determination at all costs to find the origin of tragedy in religion, and therefore in ritual. (I say "and therefore in ritual" because in a culture like that of Greece, where there are no true sacred books, the nerve center of religion is necessarily found in cult, that is, ritual.) It is curious that our secularized, "scientific" age should follow this bent so persistently. No doubt fifth-century tragedy itself, especially that of Aeschylus, is partly responsible. The plays of Aeschylus are obviously religious in the profoundest sense. Dealing with the ultimate mysteries of fate, suffering, the relation of man to god, they grip us with an overwhelming intuition of forces out of scale with human power, of titanic combats embracing earth, hell, and heaven. What more natural than to suppose that this religious drama grew out of religious ritual? Yet the inference is not necessarily valid. Aeschylus uses inherited religious forms in his plays, but their form as a whole cannot be understood as a reflection of any ritual.

Whatever the reasons, modern theorists have been almost unanimously agreed that tragedy grew out of some choral or group performance of ritual nature. It is when the next question is put—what kind of chorus, what ritual?—that the differences I have spoken of emerge.

One more presupposition has been at work in most modern speculation about the origin of tragedy, though not in such clear and unambiguous fashion as the predisposition toward ritual. I mean a pervasive assumption (more often implicit than explicit) that the origins must have been not only ritualistic but, in one way or another, *dramatic*. Here again the concrete applications diverge. Sometimes it is Thespis who is thought of as adding this element to the (undramatic) chorus, with his "actor"; sometimes the choral form itself is alleged to have been mimetic, that is, to have contained the germ of drama.[6] Unfortunately the terms "drama" and "dramatic" have several different meanings or connotations. If they are meant here as signifying direct conflict, the open clash of opposing wills, it is easy to show that such a thing is still not to be found in Aeschylus's earliest extant play;[7] and indeed it is clear on the face of it that a one-actor "drama," such as tragedy was from Thespis to Aeschylus, could not have been dramatic in this sense. If what is meant is a tension centered in the hero's tragic choice, with its foreshadowing of woe to come, that too can be shown to be just making its appearance in Aeschylus. If "dramatic" means, on the other hand, simply the presence and expression of strong emotion of almost any kind, it can be shown that the strongest emotion in the early plays is grief, not ecstasy, and that its native forms of expression are essentially static, that is, undramatic. If, finally, "dramatic" is reduced to meaning no more than "mimetic," that is, the impersonation of a character other than one's own, there is no objection to its being applied to pre-Aeschylean tragedy. But it seems to me that although such a reduction is possible with the term "dramatic," it is not possible with "drama": in other words, that when we say "drama" we do not mean less than an *action* of some kind in which people act or react upon each other. This identification of "drama" with action, something happening, is our heritage from Aristotle, and I have no quarrel with it. But we shall see later that, if the *Persians* and the *Seven Against Thebes* are any guide, Aeschylus had no such prototype before him but was still working toward the drama in the 460's.

In these remarks I have anticipated findings which will only be brought forward much later, toward the end of our investigation. I do so not only for substantive reasons, having to do with the concept of drama, but also for reasons of method. The extant plays of Aeschylus are relevant parts of the available evidence for the origin of tragedy: not that they tell us by themselves what that origin was, but that they can give us priceless clues, both positive and negative, to the literary form which Aeschylus inherited from his predecessors, and thus to some of the elements which must have belonged or cannot have belonged to that form. For this part of our undertaking we now have a firmer basis thanks to the new dating of the *Suppliants* in the 460's.[8] Previously, in default of external evidence, the leading position of the chorus in that play, combined with the gravitational pull of the *idée fixe* "choral origin of tragedy," had led most scholars to date the *Suppliants* earlier and earlier, before Salamis, even before Marathon—all this in defiance of substantial internal evidence and over strong protests from Walter Nestle.[9] Thus the *Suppliants* was taken to be a surviving specimen of a primitive form: "lyrical tragedy."[10] The matter is now settled and we can see the play as an important link in a close-knit sequence which leads from *Persians* to *Oresteia*. By the same token we are rid of the evidence it was supposed to give for choral origin.

With these prolegomena out of the way we can get down to the business of this book. The chapters follow the order of the lectures as they were delivered. The first, on "Dionysus, Goat-Men, and *Tragôidia*," is in the main a critical review of the chief theories that have been propounded from Nietzsche's day to ours. But it does not attempt to give a *catalogue raisonnée* of them all, and is not really so much concerned with the various theories *per se* as it is with the character and value of the evidence on which they rest or claim to rest. The second chapter discusses Attic culture, especially Attic literature, in the sixth century from the point of view of the matrix—spiritual, political, and technical—which it provided for the birth of the new art. The third chapter takes up the creation itself, the work of Thespis, and suggests what we know or can infer (mostly the latter) about his kind of *tragôidia*. Finally, the chapter on Aeschylus demonstrates what remained to be done before the tragic drama could be created, and sketches the process through which Aeschylus achieved it.

In fairness to the reader I will set down here, in all candor, the assumptions—he may call them biases if he prefers—which have guided me (one or two of them have been mentioned before):

1) Whatever may have happened elsewhere, in Polynesia or Peloponnese, it is Athens alone that counts.

2) The origin of tragedy was not so much a gradual, "organic" development as a sequence of two creative leaps, by Thespis and Aeschylus, with certain conditioning factors precedent to each.

3) Although the two leaps were separated from each other by a considerable space of time, the second followed in direct line from the first. There is no room between them for a reversal of the spirit of tragedy from gay to solemn.

4) There is no solid evidence for tragedy ever having been Dionysiac in any sense except that it was originally and regularly presented at the City Dionysia in Athens.

5) There is no reason to believe that tragedy grew out of any kind of possession or ecstasy (*Ergriffenheit*), Dionysiac or otherwise.

Perhaps a final word will not be out of place here. Aside from the thrill of the chase or the satisfaction of knowledge for its own sake, is it really important for us to know how and whence tragedy arose? We have some plays of the three great tragedians; are they not enough? Are they not what they are, regardless of origins? I have considerable sympathy for this point of view. But it has already been pointed out that misconceptions of the origin of Greek tragedy have led in our own time to serious misreadings of the plays themselves. Francis Fergusson's belief in Murray's "ritual sequence" led him to certain misinterpretations of the *Oedipus*; that they were not more serious we owe to his own sensitive intuition of the play, not to the theory he was following. A Stratford (Canada) performance of the *Oedipus* in 1955 was executed not only with masks but with stylized incantations and motions like the fixed routine of a ritual dance.[11] This is a fundamental misreading of Sophocles' play.

But above and beyond the negative function of averting misinterpretations of the extant ancient tragedies, I would urge that an understanding of the origin of tragedy may serve a larger humanistic purpose. Tragedy is a fashionable genre nowadays. Critics and playwrights treat it with respect; a feeling prevails among literary folk that it is the highest and somehow the "truest" literary genre; [12] a shrewd and sensitive psychologist, looking for more meaningful aesthetic experiences that could be shared by children, asks whether we might not awaken in them a response to tragedy; [13] voices are heard asking whether we can still write tragedy, and if not why not? is *Death of a Salesman* really a tragedy? etc., etc. Considering this groundswell of interest, not to say fascination,[14] it seems to me that it would be helpful for literary people generally to be aware how slender was the stem on which the tree arose in the beginning. Tragedy is a rare and special plant; not a universal form of serious literature but a unique creation born at a particular time and place. If we are to appraise it rightly, at its true value, we need to understand the circumstances and ideas which prompted its creation.

I. Dionysus, Goat-Men, and *Tragôidia*

I F ANY single impression concerning the origin of tragedy is fixed in the minds of most literate members of Western society, it is that tragedy stems from Dionysus and satyrs. This dominant impression is the joint work of as unlikely a pair of collaborators as ever lived: Aristotle and Friedrich Nietzsche.

Anyone who has read Nietzsche's *The Birth of Tragedy out of the Spirit of Music* can recall its first stunning impact upon him. The book projects with unforgettable power the rise of tragedy out of the dark womb of the "Dionysian," that indescribable, all-confounding Primal Unity of joy and pain which lies at the heart of life itself. The god of this deep substratum, where all individuation and rationality are swallowed up, is Dionysus, and its exemplar in the world of art is the satyr. Half man, half beast though the satyr is, he is nevertheless not really a lower kind of being than man. He represents in sentient form the profound truth, the primordial essence that has been glossed over by civilization. The satyr is in fact "the archetype of man, the embodiment of his highest and intensest emotions . . . wisdom's harbinger speaking from the very heart of nature." [1] Thus it is no accident that tragedy, born from the spirit of music, should have been originally incorporated in, consubstantial with, the chorus of satyrs. That chorus is "a self-mirroring of the Dionysian man," and everything that comes later—actors, action, 'drama'—is but a vision seen by it, in which the spectator (*hypocrite spectateur, son semblable, son frère*) finds his own inmost nature revealed. Through a process which Nietzsche deliberately leaves vague (the details did not interest him) the Apollonian dream world of the stage action is married to the Dionysian, "real" world of the satyr-chorus, and tragedy is born.

The Birth of Tragedy is a great book, by whatever standard one cares to measure it. For Nietzsche it was an intensely personal manifesto, in effect a farewell to *Altertumswissenschaft* and all that, the opening gun in a war whose later battles included Zarathustra and the Superman. We nowadays can see it in broader perspective, as a milestone on the *via dolorosa* which led modern man into the twentieth century. The spiritual importance of the work vastly transcends its occasion and its evidence. For us here, concerned as we are with the origin of tragedy, the remarkable thing is not the explosive revolutionary force of Nietzsche's book but its traditional and conventional basis. *The Birth of Tragedy* does not present any new theory of the origin; it simply visualizes, *visionalizes,* an outline of events suggested in Aristotle's *Poetics.* The catalyst was Wagnerian opera,[2] but the source was Aristotle. Nietzsche began, after all, as a classical scholar, and without Aristotle's phrases "those who led off the dithyramb" and "having developed out of a *satyrikon*" his "Dionysian" and his satyrs would never have come into being. Nietzsche gave these concepts new life, but he did not entirely invent them.

The Birth of Tragedy has cast a spell on almost everybody who has dealt with the subject since 1871. Even those who reject Dionysus and satyrs and look for other points of origin tend to feel—unconsciously, perhaps—that these must belong to the same order of being as Dionysus, that is, that they must go down to the deepest and most primitive levels of Greek religion. This almost universal presumption has been reinforced, I think, by two other influences. One is the intellectual trend toward primitivism which began to invade so many fields of thought around the turn of the century (not without help from Nietzsche himself). Primitivism assumed that the primitive, if not actually better than the more sophisticated, was somehow more real, potent, *urwüchsig*. The other influence is the power of the Greek tragedies themselves, especially the great religious dramas of Aeschylus. These plays, it would seem, speak the unmistakable language of Dionysiac possession, *Ergriffenheit*. Confronting such an apocalyptic vision, it is natural for the watcher to feel, "This is indeed the world of Dionysus."

Whatever the particular reasons were, the basic testimony of Aristotle (dithyramb, *satyrikon*) and the predispositions of modern students of tragedy have combined forces to locate its origin in religion, and more specifically in religious cult. Thus although the cults chosen for the purpose differ widely and the theories built on them more widely still, it is a fact that almost all the countless views put forward on the subject fix on some religious ritual—Dionysiac, Eleusinian, other agrarian, hero-cult, etc.—as the root of tragedy.

It would be a boon to the reader if we could forego an examination of these multifarious theories and get on directly to the positive argument. But it would not be a safe or a sound procedure. For better or worse, as I said in the Introduction, an impression is abroad among the general public, and even in some sectors of the scholarly world, that the question has been settled: that we know where tragedy came from and how it grew. It may be useful, then, if nothing more, to show how sparse and precarious our evidence is and how little agreement there is on the interpretation of it. And actually no new attack on the problem is likely to receive more than perfunctory attention unless such a preliminary survey has been made. In any case a new theory[3] must face the evidence sooner or later, must show what it amounts to, what it can prove and cannot prove; and this can best be achieved through an appraisal which marshals other theories in relation to the same evidence.

For these reasons we cannot avoid a survey of the field. But such a survey could not be made complete without taking up a book as long as this or longer. Hence after much thought I have limited my review to the chief *types* of theory and the evidence on which they are based. The important items of direct evidence (explicit *testimonia* concerning the origin and early stages of tragedy, together with certain statements which are traditionally associated with these) are quoted in an appendix.[4]

Tragedy, then, has been derived from three chief kinds of source: (1) The dithyramb: that is, the cult of Dionysus. With this is usually, though not always, associated the idea of a *satyrikon,* a performance by goat-like satyrs (*tragôidia = tragôn ôidê,* 'song of goats'). (2) Other orgiastic or mystery rituals more or less identifiable with or comparable to the Dionysiac: for example, the Eleusinian mysteries. This variant often goes with a desire to find a more *serious* or "tragic" source than the goat-like satyrs can provide. (3) The cult of the dead; or, to give it its specifically Greek title, hero-cult. Connected with this is an emphasis on the scenes of lamentation and the like (*thrênoi, kommoi*) in our extant tragedies.

It should be added that this threefold division is only an approximation to the inexhaustible multifariousness of the actual theories, and that combinations of elements from two or more of these categories are numerous.

Version 1 is of course the orthodox one based on the *Poetics*. Its leading advocate in this century was Wilamowitz. Version 2 involves a partial, version 3 (if consistently maintained) a total divergence from Aristotle. The best-known instance of version 2, in English-speaking countries, is Gilbert Murray's "year spirit" or *Eniautos-Daimon* theory, already mentioned in the Introduction; and the weightiest, though not the most consistent, proponent of version 3 was Martin P. Nilsson. The following survey will deal most fully with version 1, since it is the one (or ones) hallowed by tradition and the only one directly based on the *testimonia* from antiquity.

The cornerstone of the traditional version is Aristotle, *Poetics* 4,1449a9 ff.:[5] "But in any case, having developed from an improvisational beginning, both it [*sc.* tragedy] and comedy: the former from those who led off the dithyramb . . ." There can be no doubt that this refers to a choral performance, but Aristotle's words suggest that he is not thinking of the chorus itself as the prime mover, but of certain individuals[6] who stood over against the chorus and gave it a theme—as Archilochus boasts,[7] "I know how to lead off (*exarxai*) the beautiful song of lord Dionysus when my wits have been thunder-smitten with wine." It looks as though the relationship between the *exarchôn* and the dithyrambic chorus must have prefigured, in Aristotle's mind, the later relationship between actor and chorus in tragedy.[8] If so, we must guard against attaching Aristotle's name to the popular idea that the early tragic chorus was itself protagonist of the performance.

The first difficulty is to determine what kind of performance Aristotle is talking about. The fragment of Archilochus is persuasive: clearly, it would seem, we are in the realm of Dionysiac ecstasy or possession. But doubts arise from various quarters. Aristotle does not actually mention Dionysus or "the Dionysiac." In his own day the dithyramb had long since lost its Dionysiac character, to become simply a narrative poem on heroic subjects, and perhaps that is all he has in mind here in naming it as the ancestor of tragedy. Moreover, our passage shows clear parallels[9] in structure and diction with an earlier one (1448b22ff.) in which Aristotle first mentions the birth of poetry out of improvisations, and there (b27) the matrix of serious poetry is identified as hymns and encomia. Possibly, then, "dithyramb" in our passage is intended merely as a specific or generic equivalent for "hymn." The same possibility is suggested by the only other utterance we have from Aristotle concerning the earliest period. It is quoted by Themistius:[10] "(Aristotle says that) at first the chorus as it came in used to sing [*i.e.*, sing a hymn] to the gods, but Thespis invented a prologue and a (set) speech." Thus both of Aristotle's utterances on the subject are compatible with the idea that in naming the dithyramb as the ultimate source of tragedy he had in mind simply a lyric presentation of heroic subjects, not a specifically Dionysiac performance. In any case he does not emphasize or even mention Dionysus or the Dionysiac spirit. Nietzsche's evocation of *das Dionysische* is a rhapsody on a neutral theme ("those who led off the dithyramb"); it would perhaps have astonished Aristotle.

Whatever the bearing of Aristotle's testimony, there is something more to be added concerning its value. I associate myself with those[11] who refuse to accept his remarks as based on documentary evidence for the period before the beginning of the records of the dramatic festivals in Athens, probably 502/1 B.C. We know of no such evidence and find it hard to imagine what it could have been. Moreover I think I have shown elsewhere[12] that Aristotle's whole sketch of the early development of poetry in chapter 4 of the *Poetics* is shaped by an entelechic idea, that of the imitation of action, which he conceives as being caught from Homer by other poets and finally culminating in the fifth-century drama, especially tragedy. It is the same Aristotelian way of writing history that Cherniss has traced in the first book of the *Metaphysics*.[13] If that is so, what confronts us in the *Poetics* is simply another theory of the origin of tragedy; to be sure, the oldest one we know of.[14] So far as it can be grasped and understood, it deserves our respectful attention—on condition that we cease to claim it as a report of facts.[15]

The earliest name which can be placed with some probability in Aristotle's theory of the origin of tragedy is that of Arion,[16] who came from Lesbos and worked at Corinth in the early sixth century B.C. under the tyrant Periander. Herodotus tells us[17] that Arion was the first poet to "compose" a dithyramb, i.e., to write it in advance, and to give it a title and train a chorus to perform it. The giving of a title almost certainly points to heroic (epic) content, so that Arion appears as the initiator of the development which stripped the dithyramb of its specifically Dionysiac character and made it simply an heroic narrative poem. It is very likely that this is one of the most important of the "many changes" which Aristotle assigns (*Poetics* 4, 1449a14) to the development of tragedy before Aeschylus.

So much for Aristotle's theory of the growth of tragedy out of the dithyramb. It looks as though he chose the dithyramb not for its Dionysiac spirit but for precisely the opposite reason, because of all the major forms of "hymn" to the gods it was the one which did in fact begin, early in the sixth century, to lose its specific character and become a vehicle for heroic narrative in general. But this development, clear enough in itself and worth our notice as a possible route from Homer to tragedy, has been immensely complicated by the intrusion of another quite different element into the story: the satyr-chorus. It is not the dithyramb as such, it is Dionysus and the satyrs—with a mighty push from Nietzsche—that dominate our thinking and imagining in this matter.

The question of the satyrs is so complex and ramified that we shall have to deal with it at some length. But a few preliminary remarks are necessary. First, for this part of the field we have a considerable amount of visual material. We know that satyrs existed and had a role in Attic drama, and we know what they looked like. But it would never have occurred to anyone to connect them with the origin of *tragedy* if the word *satyrikon* were not found in the *Poetics*.[18] Second, the satyrs have been connected with the origin of tragedy by means of the etymology *tragôidia = tragôn ôidê,* 'song of goats,' with the accompanying idea that the satyrs were 'goats,' or goat-men. This is an indispensable link. Third, whereas derivation of tragedy from the regular dithyramb is compatible with the idea that the genre was serious from the beginning, derivation from a *satyrikon* necessarily involves a peripety in the middle of tragedy's career, a reversal from gay to grave. For let there be no mistake: Nietzsche's insinuations to the contrary, that the satyr was really a major personage, a fount of wisdom and a being in some sense superior to man, the actual satyrs of Greek legend and drama were subhuman, "good-for-nothing"[19] creatures distinguished above all by braggadocio, cowardice, and lechery. If the original tragic chorus was made up of them, tragedy must have undergone a drastic change of tone and theme somewhere along the way.

Once more we begin with Aristotle. A few lines after the passage we have already discussed he says, 1449a18 ff.:[20] "Out of small (trivial?) plots and ludicrous diction, on account of its having developed out of a (a kind of?)[21] *satyrikon*, it [sc. tragedy] acquired seriousness late." In my book on the *Poetics*[22] I argued that these words are spurious, being incoherent in themselves and inconsistent both with the surrounding context and with Aristotle's thought as a whole. I do not intend to disavow that argument here, but it would be unwise to rest our case on it until there is more sign of its being accepted. Meanwhile Webster[23] is inclined to admit that the statement about a *satyrikon,* if not spurious, at least has no direct connection with that about the dithyramb. But the two remarks are normally connected, in fact equated with each other, by those who believe in a "satyric" origin. The product of this identification is the "satyric dithyramb," a *Mischwesen* more striking than the satyrs themselves. In this case misreading of the *Poetics* is reinforced by uncritical use of an apparent piece of evidence from the Suda, concerning Arion:[24] "(He) is said also to have been the inventor of the tragic mode, and to have been the first to make a chorus stand still and to sing a dithyramb and to give a name to what was sung by the chorus, and to have brought on satyrs speaking verses." The trouble with this promising text is that although the middle part is clear enough, being very close to what Herodotus says about Arion,[25] we can neither identify the "tragic mode" nor tell for sure what the satyrs are supposed to be doing. The word "speaking" (*legontas*) is fatally inexact.[26] If Arion's satyrs had anything to do with the dithyramb they certainly did not speak, they sang. But it is not even clear that they are supposed to have anything to do with the dithyramb; it is at least as likely that these words of the Suda refer to an entirely different performance. Thus the testimony is so uncertain as to be useless.

The same must be said, but with more emphasis, about an alleged piece of evidence which Hugo Rabe uncovered[27] in a medieval commentary on Hermogenes: "The first drama [performance?] of tragedy was introduced by Arion of Methymna, as Solon set forth in the poems entitled 'Elegies.' But Dracon of Lampsacus says that a drama was first produced at Athens, composed by Thespis." As the reader can see, this testimony does not mention satyrs; but we will deal with it here while speaking of Arion. It is astonishing to see responsible scholars cite the remark as serious evidence for anything. It stands in the middle of a farrago of nonsense; "drama of tragedy" is a meaningless phrase; the word *tragôidia* itself will not go into elegiacs; we know of no Dracon of Lampsacus (Wilamowitz emended to Charon, an early Ionian logographer); it is highly unlikely that a minor annotator on Hermogenes in the 12th century A.D. had any reliable knowledge of Solon's works; and above all one cannot imagine a battle of literary claims between Athens and Peloponnese in the early sixth century,[28] much less Solon's taking part in one, and on the Peloponnesian side at that. The passage is worthless.[29]

To return to the satyrs: The urgent desire to find goat-men in Peloponnese, and early enough to supply a "tragic" prototype for Athens, has led also to unmerciful pulling and hauling on an innocent passage of Herodotus.[30] The historian records how Clisthenes, tyrant of Sicyon in the early sixth century, in the course of a war with Argos expelled the Argive (= Dorian) hero Adrastus from his grave and shrine in the market place of Sicyon. The people of Sicyon had been accustomed to give certain "honors" to Adrastus, including offerings, celebrations (festivals, *heortai*), and, in commemoration of his "sufferings" (*pathea*), "tragic choruses" (*tragikoi choroi*). Clisthenes replaced the bones of Adrastus with those of his mortal enemy, the Theban hero Melanippus, and "assigned"[31] the offerings and festivals to Melanippus, the choruses to Dionysus. These statements have been interpreted in an astonishing variety of ways, but above all the phrase *tragikoisi choroisi* has been taken to mean that the dances were performed by "goats" or goat-like satyrs. For this there is no warrant at all. As Pickard-Cambridge says,[32] aside from the unlikelihood that the honors to Adrastus were performed by ithyphallic, goat-like demons,[33] it is inconceivable that Herodotus, the friend of Sophocles and living in the great age of tragedy, should have meant anything by *tragikos* but 'tragic,' and in fact the word is not found in its strict etymological sense ("of goats, goat-like") before Plutarch. Secondly, the passage has sometimes been read as if it spoke of sufferings *of Dionysus;* but nothing of the sort is either stated or implied in it. We will come back to this point, and to the real value of Herodotus' testimony, in due time.

A satyric stage antedating tragedy proper, though without explicit identification of the satyrs as "goats," appears in one, possibly two, of the scattered notices offered in explanation of the phrase "Nothing to do with Dionysus" (*Ouden pros ton Dionyson*).[34] These notices are so confused that it is impossible to get a firm chronology out of them. But they all agree on some change of spirit and/or theme away from Dionysus; and the second explanation recorded in the Suda, the one marked as "better," identifies the older works as being "also called *satyrika.*" It can hardly be doubted that these works, written "to Dionysus," are understood to have been dithyrambs.[35] This passage, then, is the nearest thing we have to explicit ancient tetstimony for a "satyric dithyramb." And the last sentence, in spite of its ambiguity,[36] gives an important clue to the provenience of that theory, a clue to which we will return in a moment.

This completes our inventory of the literary references to the dithyramb, satyric or otherwise, as the antecedent of tragedy. We also have a considerable body of visual evidence for satyrs, chiefly on vases. But there is a serious difficulty about the use of this material. Although satyrs appear in numbers on Attic vases beginning around 520 B.C., and although many of them are clearly associated with the drama (the satyr-drama), they are regularly portrayed throughout the fifth century as horse-men, with horses' ears and tails, not as goat-men. As Lesky quaintly says,[37] the trouble is that the goats we were looking for turn out to be horses.

Here it is well to be as precise as possible. In the first place we must keep steadily in mind that our problem has to do with tragedy and therefore depends on the equation *tragôidia = tragôn ôidê,* 'song of goats.' The fifth-century satyr-drama is relevant to the question only if it can be shown that tragedy developed out of an earlier *satyrikon* and that that *satyrikon* had "goats" for choreutae. If, as many scholars think,[38] the satyr-drama was first introduced into Attica by Pratinas toward the end of the sixth century, the physiognomy and costumes of its choreutae have nothing to do with the case. They are pertinent only if they represent a survival of an earlier state of affairs *in Attica,* antedating Thespis. Second, in surveying the visual evidence for satyrs it is necessary to be sure that they do in fact represent the drama, and specifically satyr-drama (not, for example, comedy or purely imaginary satyr dances).

The evidence for satyrs has been mustered in detail by Brommer, Buschor, and more recently Webster.[39] Buschor gives a kaleidoscopic picture of satyr dances in various parts of Greece at various periods going back as far as—perhaps—the seventh century, but he pays little attention to the two principles put forward above and therefore cannot be said to have attacked our problem directly. Webster is more careful, but the most he seems to have demonstrated is that *some* fifth-century dramatic satyrs wear hairy tights which might have been ultimately derived from goat-skins, and that the fat men (padded dancers) and hairy satyrs (none of them identifiable with satyr-drama as such) who appear on various sixth-century vases from Corinth and Athens *may* have been equated with each other and

their dances could perhaps have been regarded as goat dances.[40]

The safest position with regard to the satyrs appears to be
this: Part-human, part-animal creatures of various descriptions
existed from an early date—in people's fancy—all over Greece.
'Satyr' (first found in Hesiod) [41] seems to be a generic term for
them, without specification of their exact shape or make-up.
Creatures with mixed human and caprine traits were certainly
to be found in Peloponnese. We have one (only one, from preclassical times) representation of them, showing four goat-
headed beasties dancing in a ring.[42] Their name is not given
and not known; *tragoi* and *satyroi* are possible, *Pânes* is perhaps more likely. Mixtures of human and equine also existed,
especially in the Attic-Ionic sector, and there they were usually
called 'silens' (*seilênoi*). And these creatures, with their horses'
ears and tails, became the standard choreutae of the satyr-drama, under the name *satyroi*.

Now there is no difficulty in supposing that the horse-demons
of Attic satyr-drama could share the generic term *satyroi* with
the goat-demons of Peloponnese.[43] But that is not enough to
establish the derivation of tragedy from a *satyrikon*. Here a
series of leaps is required which leave terra firma and credibility
far behind. First of all, we have to assume that a satyric dithyramb, or some kind of proto-dramatic performance involving
goat-like satyrs, existed in north Peloponnese in the time of
Clisthenes and Arion, although there is no firm evidence for
such performances at that time and no trace of them afterward. Next we are asked to believe that this "tragic" genre was
transplanted to Attica not later than the middle of the sixth
century (time of Thespis) and the following series of events
took place there: (1) Somewhere along the line from Thespis
to Aeschylus human choreutae were substituted for the old
'goats,' and this change together with the introduction of a
first actor (by Thespis) initiated the development which led to
tragedy as we know it. (2) Meanwhile, or subsequently (it is

really impossible to date this part of the process, bceause everything depends on one's view of when and why and how the
satyr-drama as such was introduced), the old play with the goat-
men was continued—or re-established—[44] alongside tragedy;
but (3) the goat-men were now, as a normal thing, changed into horse-men but still called *satyroi,* while (4) the term 'goat-
song' (*tragôidia*) was retained as the enduring title not of
satyr-drama but of the other genre, the one which hencefor-
ward had nothing to do with either goat-men or horse-men.

If the foregoing reads like a parody or a phantasmagoria, it
is not my fault. The plain fact is that the whole tragedy-out-of-
satyrikon theory reduces itself to chaotic nonsense the moment
one tries to apply it to the known history of tragedy *in Attica.*
The crux of the difficulty lies in Thespis. We will deal with
Thespis in his own right in the third chapter; all that is needed
here is to observe that in the direct tradition about him there is
nothing whatever to connect him either with satyrs, goat-like
or otherwise, or with the dithyramb.[45] All such connections are
corollaries—necessary ones, if we are determined to find the
origin of tragedy in Peloponnese—of the *satyrikon* theory.

Whence all these difficulties? They come from trying to su-
per-impose a prehistory of tragedy in the Peloponnese upon a
history in Attica which is complete and coherent in itself.[46] And
this overloading of the story is not an accident. It stems from
an attempt by certain "Dorians" in the late fourth century B.C.
to annex the origins of both tragedy and comedy. Evidence for
the attempt is on view in the third and fourth chapters of the
Poetics. I pointed out in my analysis of the argument in chapter
3[47] that, far from being neutral toward the Dorian claims to
comedy, as he is usually said to be, Aristotle implicitly fav-
ors them. His discussion there tends to direct the major emphasis toward comedy and the claims that were laid to it by the
two Megaras. The claim to tragedy is only mentioned in the
briefest way, as pressed by "some of those in Peloponnese." But
other testimony makes clear what would be evident anyhow,

that he means Corinth and Sicyon: the work of Arion and, probably, Epigenes.[48]

This is not to say that Aristotle held the *satyrikon* theory. I
still maintain my bracketing of the words in chapter 4, 1449a18-
21, including the phrase "out of a *satyrikon*."[49] This leaves
untouched the statement a line or two later, a22: "For initially
they used the (trochaic) tetrameter on account of the composition being satyr-like, that is, pretty much just dancing"; but
this clearly refers to the mode of composition of early tragedy,
not to the constitution of the chorus. I would also reiterate and
in fact strengthen what was said in my book about the earlier
passage, 1449a9-11, on the dithyramb, and especially about the
general spirit and point of Aristotle's brief "history" of tragedy.
His narrative records an entelechic growth toward perfection,
beginning with a split in the body of poetry between *spoudaion*
and *geloion,* serious and ludicrous.[50] This division is so fundamental to Aristotle's thinking that a contravention of it, such
as would necessarily be involved in any development of tragedy
out of a *satyrikon,* appears to me strictly incredible. I would
therefore emphasize more than I did in my book the parallel
between his mention of the dithyramb and his earlier allusion
to the period of improvisation, 1448b27, where he says that serious poetry sprang from hymns and encomia. The old dithyramb was a form of hymn, and Arion's introduction of heroic
content into it would make it in effect a kind of encomion. I
suggest that this is Aristotle's real meaning in the *Poetics,* and
that it excludes satyrs, though it does not exclude a "satyr-like"
style or form of composition in which dancing predominated.

So much for Aristotle's own theory. It certainly included
Arion at Corinth and Epigenes and/or other poets at Sicyon. In
other words it assigned a key role in the development of tragedy
to Dorian lands, just as it gave to Dorian poets, especially Epicharmus, a key role in the development of comedy. But there
were men close to Aristotle in the Lyceum who were, I think,
not content with this. In my book it was suggested that the

Dorian claims mentioned in chapter 3 of the *Poetics* had been formulated, at least in part, by those professional Dorians Dicaearchus and (and/or) Aristoxenus. I further suggested, somewhat hesitantly, that the interpolated matter in chapter 4, 1449a17-21, came from Chamaeleon or someone influenced by him. I now wish to renew this latter suggestion, and on a broader base.

The whole idea of a competition between Dorian and Athenian claims to the origination of the drama could only have arisen in the fourth century and in the context of Aristotle's school.[51] For not only was it he who had shown the way to the serious study of *Literaturgeschichte,* it was he who had reversed Plato's verdict on the drama, especially tragedy, and established it as the supreme literary genre. His work and ideas inspired several generations of Peripatetics to literary scholarship on an unheard-of scale[52] and with results and aftereffects which have been truly global, from the Library of Alexandria to the latest *History of English* (*Portuguese, Mongol, Javanese,* etc.) *Literature.* The Peripatetic *Literaturhistoriker* followed their master's lead but were not necessarily bound by his particular opinions. Aside from keenness of mind and unflagging zeal in research, or at least in the collection of material, they had one thing in common: hardly any of them were Athenians. The Lyceum, unlike the Academy and the schools of rhetoric, was a nest of foreigners.

This paradox of a non-Athenian (and for "non-" we may read in some cases "anti-") school of literary studies at work in the heart of Athens, the literary capital of Greece, deserves a treatment of its own which cannot be given here. The anti-Athenian bias differs in degree from member to member but often turns up even where it is irrelevant or inappropriate. The great rallying point and slogan for such activities was "Dorian." "Ionian" had gone down the drain of history; its rebirth was to come later, in Alexandrian times. "Aeolic" was an honorable name but included too little of crucial importance—in particular, no drama. "Dorian" offered the best hopes for literary chauvinism against Athens, and Aristotle had defined tragedy as the supreme literary achievement, even above Homer. How then to annex tragedy for the Dorian cause?

One fatal fact stood in the way. The Dorian peoples did indeed possess a number of ancient and well-marked varieties of *comic* drama—Corinthian padded dancers, Laconian *bryllichistai* and *deikêliktai,* Epicharmus, Sophron, etc.—, but they had nothing remotely resembling tragedy. Tragedy was a peculiarly and uniquely Athenian invention, from Thespis to Theodectes.

One procedure was to allege theft by Athenian from non-Athenian dramatists. The type-case is the feeble allegation that Euripides stole his *Medea* from the insignificant Neophron.[53] But not much could be accomplished that way, if only because there were so few tragedians who could even be claimed as Dorian. The only practicable major route of attack was via the beginnings. If Thespis could be outflanked, made to depend on early Dorian precedents and inventions, the game could be won.[54] Aristotle had shown the way with his references to the dithyramb, to Corinth and Sicyon. But that was too limited, and his rigid distinction between serious and "trivial" genres was only a hindrance. What if all drama, comedy, satyr-drama *and* tragedy, could be derived from a single root? Then it could all be Peloponnesian, that is, Dorian, in origin. The idea is Peripatetic, though we cannot identify its author. What we find in *Poetics* 4, 1449a17-21, is one offshoot of it, just as the name Susarion marks an attempt to annex Athenian comedy to Dorian Megara.[55] Here the *satyrikon* provides the magic key. Tragedy arose out of "small plots"—a phrase which, whatever its supposed application to tragedy, would do very well as a description of the plots of both comedy and satyr-play—and "ludicrous (= comic) diction," and only grew serious ("sobered up" would not be an inappropriate translation) late in its career. All this is very close to the assertion reported by Plutarch,[56] that tragedy and comedy both arose "out of laughter." The

Plutarch passage speaks to the theme "nothing to do with Dionysus," like the ones we cited earlier,[57] and similarly reports a drastic change from gay to grave. We are in the same country as before.

The Dorianizing solution (which had to assume, be it noted, either a satyric or a comic origin: Peloponnese had nothing else to show) is no solution. It is certain that Attic comedy and tragedy had quite different origins,[58] and almost as certain that satyr-drama was brought to Athens by Pratinas at the end of the sixth century.[59] Its introduction into the tragic competition was a response to some kind of popular protest against a steady diet of death and disaster[60] (Athenians were not so different from other people in wanting to laugh occasionally), and there are indications that it was some time before the procedure settled down to the later fifth-century ratio of three tragedies to one satyr-play, all written by the same poet.[61] Thus satyr-drama had an origin of its own, although it ended by becoming a satellite of tragedy, and we are no longer bound, 2300 years later, to accept the pro-Dorian propaganda of Chamaeleon and his confrères.

It should also be said at this point that *tragôidia,* whatever its original meaning and application, is proved by its vocalism (*tragaoidia* > *tragôidia*: contraction *aoi* > *ôi*) to be an Attic word,[62] and since we never find it anywhere except in Athens until after the spread of Attic drama over Greece, the most natural thing is to suppose that it was coined there. Secondly, although this has been generally ignored in discussions of the matter, the equation *tragôidia* = *tragôn ôidê,* 'song of goats,' which as we saw is the necessary prop of the tragedy-out-of-*satyrikon* theory, is linguistically impossible. A word *tragôidê* (*trag-ôidê*) does not exist, and neither is there an *-ôidia* which might have been compounded with *trag-*. *Tragôidia* is a regular type of secondary compound, from the primary compound *tragôidos* (*-oi*), like *rhapsôidia, parôidia* from *rhapsôidos, parôidos*. In these compounds the first part regularly denotes the

content or circumstances of the singing; certainly not the singer.[63] In other words the Peloponnesian "goats," even if they
had given rise to tragedy, could not have been dubbed *tragôidoi,* goats who were singers or singers who were goats. Finally it must be pointed out that in the sixth century, when the
terms we are discussing were invented, *âidein (aeidein),* 'sing,'
and *ôidos (aoidos),* 'singer,' were still intimately associated with
the recitation of epic poetry. Whether the epics were still actually sung at that time, or merely chanted in some kind of re-
citative, is not to the point. They had been sung in the past, and
the hallowed words *aeidein* and *aoidos* still clung to them. In
fact I would argue that in the sixth century *aoidos* or *-ôidos* was
more likely to suggest recitation by an individual than singing
by a group.[64]

Our survey so far has turned up no incontrovertible evidence
for either the dithyramb proper or the hypothetical "satyric
dithyramb" having been the forerunner of tragedy. Rather it
appears that Aristotle's brief remarks on the dithyramb were
expressions of a theory which we are not necessarily bound to
accept; and we have seen reason to believe that the *satyrikon*
was injected into the discussion for a particular polemical reason, and not by Aristotle himself. As we turn to the second
group of theories, based not on Aristotle or the ancient *testimonia* but on various kinds of archaeological and anthropological evidence,[65] it becomes increasingly difficult to keep our
bearings and maintain any unity in the account; indeed it
might be questioned whether the word "group" is in order at
all. But it is true that a number of theories have been put forward in the last generation or two which, though not necessarily bound to the dithyramb, the satyrs, or any of the other
standard gambits, nevertheless keep some connection with Dionysus, either as god of vegetation or as patron of drunkenness
or ecstasy (*"Ergriffenheit"*) or as representative of the species
'dying god'[66] (even, as some put it, the 'hero' among the
gods).[67] Common to these attempts is a tendency to give com-

parative, anthropological material preference over specifically Greek evidence, and to view "Dionysus" in broader perspective and in a more somber, "tragic" light than the traditional theory. Thus we find that although we have disposed of the goat-men we have not yet got rid of Dionysus. He lurks athwart our path in many disguises, not least in that of the suffering god or hero.

Such approaches avoid one prime difficulty of the *satyrikon-*theory, the peripety from gay to tragic. They assume that tragedy was tragic in some sense from the beginning. They also avoid, in varying degrees, the dichotomy Dorian-Athenian. But they pay the penalty for these avoidances in vagueness and lack of contact with what little we know about the early development of tragedy in Athens.

Most prominent of these theories, in the English-speaking world, has been the *schema* associated with the name of Gilbert Murray.[68] Murray professed to find in the extant Greek tragedies extensive traces of a primitive ritual sequence which could also be confirmed by anthropological parallels: a *Ludus Sacer* celebrating the *pathê* or sufferings of an *Eniautos-Daimon* or Year-Spirit. This spirit is identified with Dionysus, with Osiris, and more generally still with the multifarious divinities grouped by Sir James Frazer under the heading of 'The Dying God.' The ritual sequence in question represents the annual death and rebirth of the *daimôn,* in six stages: *Agôn* or Contest (Winter against Summer, old year against new year), *Pathos* (ritual or sacrificial death of the god), Messenger's Speech ("the Great Pan is dead," etc.), *Thrênos* or lamentation, *Anagnorisis* (recognition of the slain and mutilated *daimôn*), and *Theophany* (his resurrection and apotheosis or epiphany to his worshippers). Obviously, although the sequence ends with an "extreme change of feeling," a peripety, as Murray calls it, from grief to joy, the tonality from beginning to end is serious, tragic. It deals all the way through with the sufferings of "Dionysus."

Unfortunately there is no proof of the existence of such a

ritual sequence anywhere in the Greek world, and the attempt to apply it to the extant plays was a tissue of *non-sequitur*'s and *petitiones principii*. The errors were examined in detail by Pickard-Cambridge thirty-five years ago, and it is time that they ceased to haunt us. The whole idea appears to have sprung initially from a misreading of the passage in Herodotus about the *tragikoi choroi* at Sicyon, as if it said that they portrayed the sufferings of Dionysus, whereas it clearly means that they dealt with the *pathê* of Adrastus and were subsequently transferred to Dionysus: the songs, not the sufferings. Actually the fortune of Murray's theory was due to its shrewd combination of certain features from the plays with the alleged anthropological evidence. The extant tragedies are indeed full of combats, deaths, and messenger's speeches, but the form and order in which these appear have nothing to do with an inherited ritual sequence. There is sufficient refutation of Murray in the simple fact that for at least its first thirty or forty years, from *ca.* 534 to 500 or later, tragedy had only one actor. Ritual drama, especially one involving contests and combats, cannot make do with a single actor,[69] and it is inconceivable that if it began with two or more it would have reduced them to one. The fact is that Murray—and the procedure is characteristic of this kind of theory—never tried to apply his scheme to Thespis or to any part of the actual Athenian development down to Aeschylus.

Farnell[70] derived tragedy from ritual combats between Black Man and Fair Man in the cult of Dionysus Eleuthereus, which had been imported to Athens by Pisistratus. Ridgeway[71] suggested that tragedy originated in dramatic dances associated with hero-cult but these rites were later absorbed into the cult of Dionysus. With him, however, we are really beginning to move toward our third category, for hero-cult is in fact a cult of the dead (the great or important dead), involving the ritual apparatus of lamentation among other things, and Ridgeway devoted an entire chapter of his book to the *thrênoi* and similar manifestations in the extant Greek plays. Likewise Dieterich[72] saw tragedy as derived from a *thrênos* for the hero. The difference was in the way they established the connection with tragedy as we know it. Ridgeway did this by assuming that the lamentations for heroes were everywhere absorbed into the cult of Dionysus (on the model of the development at Sicyon mentioned by Herodotus), while Dieterich preferred to modulate in the direction of Athens and Thespis by way of the sacred *drômena* in the cult of Demeter at Eleusis and the festival of the Anthesteria.

This leads us at last to Martin Nilsson, whose essay of 1911[73] remains a fundamental contribution to the entire subject. Nilsson offered a survey of the Greek *thrênos* over its double course of development, in life and in literature, and gave weighty reasons for considering it a constituent element of tragedy. Along the way he dealt hearty blows to the *satyrikon* theory. But then he felt obliged to take account of Dionysus after all, and ended by postulating a cult lamentation by a chorus of *tragoi* (*not* satyrs) over the slain goat which is the ritual embodiment of Dionysus.

The weakness of any theory based on hero-cult is that we can neither identify any dramatic or protodramatic performances at the tombs of Greek heroes, unless in the case of Adrastus at Sicyon, nor find any specific connection between them on the one hand and the drama in Athens on the other. The difficulties and discrepancies rise to a critical pitch—as they do under all current theories—when one tries to fit Thespis into the development. For it is just in Athens and in connection with Thespis that the possible role of hero-cult in the story as a whole is least clear. On the other hand Dieterich and Nilsson could point to one concrete and impressive feature of the extant plays, particularly the plays of Aeschylus, namely the frequency of *thrênoi* and scenes of mourning. Thus theories based on the *thrênos* do at least provide some link with the earliest extant drama, and that is more than can be said of those which begin with dithyramb, *satyrikon,* or any other ritual base.

As we conclude this review of the theories that have been put forward and the evidence (mostly alleged evidence) on which they are based, I want to return to Dionysus for a moment. The magnetic pull of his cult and, one may say, of his personality, is clearly very strong. Although many scholars have rejected the dithyramb-*satyrikon* gambit and looked to other quite different kinds of source for tragedy, it is noteworthy how many of these turn out to be "Dionysus" after all, though in a more elastic sense. Even some proponents of hero-cult and *thrênos* feel an obligation to re-establish the link with Dionysus one way or another. It appears that we could say of Dionysus what Horace said of nature: "Expelles furca, tamen usque recurret." And indeed the situation is basically the same; for in this context Dionysus *is,* in a very important sense, "nature."

Here we come back to Nietzsche; for in spite of the conventional base that served as underpinning for his theory, the import of the vision he projects is the Dionysiac spirit, and that spirit is what survives, sometimes in bizarre ways, in most of the speculations on the origin of tragedy, even from scholars who owe nothing directly to Nietzsche. Against it I must reiterate what was said in the Introduction, that there is no plausible reason to believe that tragedy was ever Dionysiac in any respect except that Pisistratus attached it, once and for all, to his festival of the Greater Dionysia.[74] Why he did so, what purpose he had in mind, is a question that will concern us later. Meanwhile it is appropriate to say a little more about Dionysus here, under two headings: the spirit of tragedy, and its content.

The spirit of Dionysus is Protean, infinitely diverse yet single: lop off a limb here and he will grow a new one there. And there is no doubt that Nietzsche caught and characterized the essential thing about that spirit: that it is ecstatic, irrational, self-contradictory, wild, refractory to discipline, gay yet menacing, eternally the same yet eternally the other. Lesky speaks for many scholars when he identifies the Dionysiac ecstasy,

Ergriffenheit, as the root of the tragic drama. Yet he himself speaks of the *"logos*-bound world of tragedy,"[75] and I would insist on that distinction. Nothing either in the traditions about Thespis or in the extant plays, earlier or later, shows any trace of the "Dionysiac ecstasy." Peretti[76] has shown that the actors' speeches in the earliest extant plays follow a strict rational pattern, dry rather than emotional: no touch of *Ergriffenheit* in them. And when the choruses reach a high point of emotion, their feelings are either *fear*[77] or *grief*—not ecstasies, Dionysiac or other.

The same thing has to be said about the content. Dionysiac subjects account for only a small proportion of Aeschylus' plays, and where Dionysus did appear there is reason to think that he was presented unsympathetically, or at least as a problem.[78] We have no indication that Aeschylus wrote as his devotee, any more than he wrote as a partisan of Demeter.

But, it will be said, all this is in the fifth century; it was very different a hundred years earlier. Perhaps it was; no one can prove that it was not. But it needs to be repeated over and over again, with emphasis, that nothing in the tradition about the early history of tragedy *in Attica* requires us to assume Dionysiac content for Thespis[79] or for any other stage in the process. And as I said at the beginning, Attica is the only place that counts. The literary developments in Peloponnese (Corinth and Sicyon) which are alleged to have led to tragedy not only did not lead to anything resembling tragedy in the Peloponnese itself; they left no subsequent trace of their own existence, no tradition that can be affiliated in any way with serious drama. The cardinal fact remains that Athens in the sixth century B.C. is the only place in the world that has ever given birth to tragedy. We must now take a closer look at that Athens.

II. Solon and Pisistratus: The Attic Matrix

I F TRAGEDY is the unique child of sixth-century Athens, it ought to be possible to gain some clues to its origin by surveying her literary, intellectual, and religious life during that period, to see what it was about Athens that might have suggested or fostered the new creation. But a survey of this kind has to be guided by some idea, if only as a heuristic device. What is it we are looking for?

In brief, we are not looking for another kind of chorus to substitute for the satyrs; and we are not looking for a previous form, literary or religious, out of which tragedy "developed." We are on the watch for events, situations, institutions, ideas, which might have induced or encouraged the invention of a peculiar new literary genre. This genre was a mixed affair, involving the self-presentation of a hero[1] in iambic and/or trochaic verses, before a chorus, and in a spirit which was grave if not actually tragic. Its content came, we are assuming, from epic sources, but the speeches of the hero were shaped by the elegiac and iambic as well as the epic tradition.

It will be noticed that nothing is said here about 'drama.' I have already spoken in the Introduction about the danger of presuming that early tragedy was "dramatic"—which begs the question by assuming as known what we are trying to find out. For our purposes 'drama' is a red herring.[2] If we look for drama in sixth-century Athens, not only shall we not find it, we shall be looking for something that was still not completely there in 472 when Aeschylus wrote the *Persians*. On the other hand, giving up the hunt for 'drama' has positive benefits to offer. It opens up our mental focus to include certain other things which are of the first importance: things such as the mode of self-presentation and the sense of tragedy, without which the tragic drama never could have—never has—come into being.

The life of sixth-century Athens is known to us very incompletely and imperfectly. The historical evidence is thin, and there is nothing to compare with the golden flood of literary source material that pours out of the fifth century: the plays of Aeschylus, Sophocles, Euripides, and Aristophanes; the histories of Herodotus and Thucydides; Plato's recollections of his youth; the beginnings of oratory, etc. Actually the only extant Athenian literature from the sixth century, except—perhaps— a Homeric hymn or two and a few traditional drinking songs, is something less than three hundred lines of Solon's poetry, most of it fragments. This fact is not accidental; it is significant. Aside from the shadowy Thespis and his equally shadowy successor Choerilus, Solon is the only Athenian poet or man of letters whom we can even name from the whole sixth century. It is not that the works of the others are lost; there were no others. Solon *is* Athenian literature, down to Aeschylus, except for the beginnings of tragedy itself.

Solon was, of course, not primarily a literary person but a public man, a statesman.[3] Though later generations tended to glorify him with one voice as the founder of Athenian democracy, or, in the case of the moderate conservatives, of the "ancestral constitution," he was far from commanding such unqualified devotion during his own life. The Attica in which he grew up, in the latter part of the seventh century, was a land riven by political and social dissensions, and this bitter *stasis,* although it gave Solon scope for his greatest achievements, also sharpened his awareness of his own distinctness from both the contending factions and left him at the end a lonely, almost a tragic, figure.

The Athenian nobles of Solon's day, the Eupatrids or "men of good fathers," were a single-minded crew of hard-riding, high-living country squires, given to sport and hunting, lovers

of horseflesh and good wine, proud of their pedigrees and un-
troubled by the slightest doubt of their God-given right to the
land and all the goods that sprang from it, including political
power. Indeed political life, social and religious life, and, most
important of all for an agricultural community, the land itself,
were exclusively in their hands. They could have paraphrased
Louis XIV's *bon mot* and said, "L'Etat, c'est nous." We shall
not go far wrong in thinking of them as very like their contemporary, the Lesbian aristocrat Alcaeus, though less talented.
And like Alcaeus and Greek aristocrats in general, they had no
squeamishness about wealth, possessions, *chrêmata*. The great
Dipylon vases of the eighth century[4] give us a vivid idea of
the wealth and pride of this nobility, especially in connection
with its funerals.

Solon's longest extant poem, the so-called "Prayer to the
Muses,"[5] begins with a plea for wealth and reputation: "Shin-
ing children of Memory and Olympian Zeus, Pierian Muses,
hear my prayer. Grant me from the blessed gods wealth, and
from mankind ever to enjoy good repute." And he goes on to
sketch a vivid picture of how wealth given by the gods remains
secure, solidly planted forever, while that which men seek in a
spirit of wanton pride comes to them unwillingly and is followed sooner or later by the vengeance of Zeus: "for no man
who has an evil heart ever escapes *his* watchful eye, and one
way or another in the end his justice is made manifest."

There can be no doubt that Solon has the nobles in mind
when he speaks of the indiscriminate lust for wealth, for in another poem he castigates "the unrighteous mind of the leaders
of the people . . . they do not know how to hold their greed
in check."[6] These "leaders of the people" are of course the nobility. Through their rapacity a good proportion of the free-
holders of Attica had lost their land and even their freedom,
through foreclosure of mortgages secured on the person of the
borrower. At some time between 594 and 590 the strife between
haves and have-nots in Attica came to the verge of open civil

war, and Solon was elected "arbitrator [or reconciler] and chief magistrate." [7] Then, as he himself wrote later, he "held his shield over both parties," fighting both on behalf of both, with the result that they both turned on him and he found himself "at bay like a wolf among many hounds" [8]—a Homeric simile with a very un-Homeric application. This is not the place to discuss Solon's political and economic reforms; what concerns us is his thoughts, his motives, and his reactions to the new and perilous situation in which he found himself. Solon was no leveler. He pitied the wretchedness of the common folk and was indignant at the callous greed of their exploiters. But "I have given the people so much privilege as suffices them, neither robbing them of their rights nor holding out the hope of more; and for those who had power and were looked up to for their wealth, I took care that they too suffer nothing unseemly." [9] In other words Solon had no intention of overturning the traditional balance of nobles and commoners. But their relationships were to be governed by justice, the justice which underlies Zeus's governance of the world and is the only solid basis for human government as well.

Solon's description of *eunomia,* the reign of law, which "dims wanton pride, makes crooked judgments straight, softens arrogant deeds, and brings acts of sedition to an end," [10] is broad in spirit but intensely practical. He saw law and reason not as distant godlike forms but as the cement that holds the body politic together. His twin goals were freedom and unity for Attica. But he saw that freedom can only be guaranteed by law and unity can only be based on reasonable consent. Solon stands forth as the first discoverer of that inner balance which has remained the life principle of free societies ever since, between freedom and responsibility, consent and authority, the morally autonomous individual and the demands of society. The verses in which he proclaims how he had held his shield over both parties and would let neither win more than it was entitled to, attest his faith in the justice of Zeus, but also in something more difficult to define, in a sense more abstract, yet perfectly concrete: a potential unity, a point of balance which was not within the domain of either Athenian party but embraced them both. In this difficult faith, this wise dreaming, Solon is unique among the poets of archaic Greece, equally remote from the truculent individualism of an Archilochus, the high-born *insouciance* of an Alcaeus, and the embittered class-consciousness of a Theognis. Solon is sturdily and indefeasibly concentrated upon social and political *reality*—a reality none the less real for being hard to discern among the distractions of party strife. And this concentration is peculiarly Athenian.[11]

Solon's conviction about the reality of *eunomia* is also basically religious; it is a faith in things unseen, unapparent, seemingly nonexistent, to a superficial eye. But this faith is not in any way visionary or mystical. It has to do with real things like Earth, the Attic earth out of which he had removed the mortgage stones for debt,[12] and the concrete blessings of law and concord in a political society. Above all, it does not proceed from any divine revelation or cult. Solon is not recorded to have enjoyed a visitation from any god. His faith is his own achievement, a product of his own intelligence and reflection on his experience. In this respect he could not be more different from the Boeotian Hesiod, to whom the Muses—*his* Muses— had revealed the truth on the summit of Mt. Helicon,[13] or from the Hebrew prophets. Solon has no laurel staff, no consecration. He prays to the Muses, but in how different a spirit from the accredited bard! He himself says, wistfully, "Any way you turn, the mind of the immortals is hidden to men."[14] Solon is equally removed from the professionalism of the epic singer, whose art in itself gives him the prerogative of special commerce with the Muses and special knowledge of the gods, and the self-abandonment of the religious votary, at one with his god in the moment of ecstasy.

This specifically Attic religiosity of Solon, his religious view of the structure of life (political and communal as well as individual) won through personal experience and hard personal meditation, without benefit of revelation or cult, is not merely an archaic parallel to the religiosity of the fifth-century tragedians (particularly Aeschylus and Euripides; Sophocles is harder to categorize); it is their prototype. Nowhere else in archaic or classical Greece do we find this strange mixture of religious individualism and responsibility; nowhere else does the individual poet presume to speak to his people about the gods on his own responsibility, on the basis of his own unassisted wrestling with the problem. The parallels in other Greek lands are rather with philosophers (Pythagoras, Parmenides, Empedocles, Heraclitus), and there the pose is usually hieratic, the content of the message a divine *logos*.[15]

In one sense the religious affinity between Solon and his Athenian successors is a commonplace. Everyone knows how close Solon's theodicy, as stated in the "Prayer to the Muses," is to the religious thinking of Aeschylus: the same conviction that crime is punished in the end, the same belief in the solidarity of the generations. But it is important here not to overreach the evidence and misinterpret the relationship. There is no evidence to prove or compelling reason to make us assume that tragedy was "theological" before Aeschylus, who began to write two full generations after Solon's death. Indeed, as we shall see later, there is no compelling reason to assume that Aeschylus' own early work was markedly theological. What is decisive for the history of tragedy is not a continuity in religious belief, or even in the posing of theological problems (who can imagine that Phrynichus was much interested in theology?), but a continuity of *mode,* posture, in the relation of the poet to the gods. When the tragic poet, in the person of Aeschylus, began to brood on the divine principles that underlie the patterns of tragic suffering (and there is every reason to believe that it was Aeschylus who first did so, at a certain stage in his career and for certain reasons), is it not evident that he had no guidance from cult,[16] no *schema* available from any source outside himself—in short, that he had to break new ground and go through the whole painful process by his own effort and on his own responsibility? When he did so, as an Attic poet, it was natural that he should follow the lead given by Solon, the Attic pioneer in such matters; though that was only the beginning. But the crucial point for the beginnings of tragedy is that it inherited no model or pattern of exegesis from cult or any other religious source. If there had been such a model in the tradition, Aeschylus could hardly have ignored it.[17]

A kindred feature of Solon's poetry is the total absence of mythology. Partly this belongs to the style of elegiac and iambic poetry; partly, no doubt, it reflects the sober, present-oriented temper of Solon's own mind. But surely it cannot be dissociated, either, from the relative poverty of Attica in myths. Whatever the ultimate reasons, Attica had less major mythology or legend attached to it than any other part of mainland Greece between Pagasae and Cape Taenarum.[18] The only quasi-mythical being who appears in Solon's poetry is Mother Earth herself; and here, though she is the traditional consort of Heaven and mother of the gods, she is also the soil of Attica, the body on which Solon had performed his healing surgery.

This quasi-vacuum or low density of mythological tradition in Attica was perhaps in the long run her greatest asset for the development of a tragic drama based on myth; for it meant that her poets were free to choose those myths that best suited the tragic idea, without regard to their status in local tradition, that is, their pre-established appeal to Attic pride or piety. Thus Athens was uniquely fitted to become what she in fact became in the fifth century: residual legatee and reinterpreter of the pan-Hellenic stock of myth for the whole Greek nation. She did this, in the persons of her great poets from Aeschylus onward, by virtue of *a new penetration of the myths from within,* a new way of facing directly up to them and asking their general import in terms of human experience.[19] This would have been much more difficult if tragedy had begun with accredited Attic myths, and next to impossible if it had been committed at the beginning to a particular body of myths necessarily slanted toward a particular interpretation, such as the alleged "sufferings of Dionysus."

After Solon had completed his great work of arbitration and settlement, tradition records that he laid down his office and went abroad on prolonged travels.[20] After his return to Attica, and in the evening of his life, he had to face the present danger of a thing which he had rejected for himself and against which he had warned his fellow-citizens in vain: the "tyranny" of Pisistratus. Thus it might seem that the structure which he had labored to establish had fallen apart. But this was only a passing appearance. The Attic yeomen remained free, Solon's basic constitutional reforms endured and were reaffirmed after the expulsion of the Pisistratids, and the mortgage stones were gone forever. Smiling vineyards and olive groves were Earth's enduring testimony to her liberation. Above all, the spirit of Solon lived on in the combination of freedom and responsibility that characterized Athens at her best, during the Persian Wars and at the height of the Periclean Age. Classical Athens was the child of Solon more than of any other single man.

We come now to an aspect of Solon's work which is even more closely connected with our theme. He was not only the greatest statesman of archaic Athens, he was her greatest and only literary man. A certain amount of ink has been spilled, to little purpose, over the question whether Solon was a great poet. Whether he was or not, he was a born writer, a man who felt an insistent need to communicate his thoughts and feelings to more men than happened to be within range of his voice at the moment, and beyond the immediate issues of the moment. Moreover, although he treasured the "good things" of life all his days—love, friendship, wine, horses and dogs—[21] most of his writing centered on public questions. Nowadays much of it would be called—ugly word!—"journalistic." In any case its

predominant aim was persuasion and, in a higher sense, in-
struction. These aims are thoroughly in keeping with the spirit
of Ionian elegy, and Solon seems to have done his first writing
in elegiac couplets. Elegy was the accepted medium for *parainesis,* exhortation or counsel, in the seventh century.[22] Solon certainly knew most of the extant examples of the form, the work
of Callinus, Archilochus, Mimnermus, perhaps Tyrtaeus, and
he must have heard and even composed many a new one at the
symposia during his *Wanderjahre.*

Such elegies were essentially personal statements on a mooted
or traditional theme: the duty of a citizen on the battlefield;
the relative value of health, wealth, and "virtue;" the cheerless-
ness of old age; and so on. But the personal note was kept within limits. In verse form, diction, and temper, elegy is the closest
of all Greek poetic forms to the impersonal epic. Archilochus is
clearly less "Archilochian," less vituperative and openly personal, in his elegiac than in his iambic and trochaic verses, and
Mimnermus's elegiacs do not tell us much about the poet as an
individual. Solon's "Prayer to the Muses" falls within this par-
aenetic tradition of the elegy. The other great poem we know
of from his early years was also in elegiacs, but here we can de-
tect a growing tension between form and content. "Salamis"
dates from somewhere in the last years of the seventh century.[23] The Athenians, having failed to capture or recapture
Salamis from the Megarians, had forbidden anyone to propose
a resumption of the war. Solon, we are told, his patriotic spirit
galled by the edict, feigned madness, then burst into the market place with a cap—a traveler's cap, it appears—on his head,
and recited an elegiac poem of his own composition, calling for
a crusade to win back the island.[24] The stratagem was success-
ful and Solon's fame was established (perhaps also that of
Pisistratus, who according to some authorities won his first
military honors in the campaign).[25] The details of the story
may have been spun out of the poem itself; but even the eight
lines we possess, out of the original one hundred, clearly show

the strength of Solon's feeling and prove the basic point, namely that his action involved *impersonating another man in a
public situation*: "I have come myself as a herald from longed-
for [or desirable] Salamis, having composed a poem, a sequence
of verses, instead of a speech" [i.e., a poem was not expected on
such an occasion]. And "On that day [i.e., on any day when
Athens gives up Salamis for good] may I change my fatherland and become a citizen of Pholegandros or Sikinos [insig-
nificant Aegaean islands]; for straightway there would be talk
among men, 'This fellow is an Athenian, one of the Salamis-
droppers.' " [26]

Elsewhere[27] I cited this episode as the beginning of a "his-
trionic period" in Athenian history, in which however, as it
turned out, the acting honors were won by Pisistratus. I would
not wish to overemphasize the suggestion. In any case the discovery Solon had made was not lost on him, namely that poetry
could be used in a new and direct way, in a kind of dialogue
between himself and his fellow citizens on a crucial occasion.

The Salamis episode took place when Solon was a young
man. He continued to write elegies in later life. But after his
archonship—no doubt some time after, in view of his travels—
he found it necessary to defend himself and his work. Solon
attacked the problem with his customary energy, in several
poems perhaps spread over several years. Some of them were
in elegiac meter, like the one I have already quoted on his due
apportionment of rights and honors to both parties. But he
also fitted new and sharper arrows to his bow. One poem begins (as we have it from Aristotle, and it is possible that it did
in fact begin so) abruptly, with a rhetorical question: "And I,
when I brought the people together for certain purposes, why
did I stop before achieving them? To these things *she* can
best bear witness in the court [or: process, court-case] of Time,
great mother of Olympian gods, black Earth, from whom I
once removed the boundary-stones that were stuck in her at
many places; she who was formerly enslaved but now is free."

And the passage, or the poem, ends with the proud statement that he had given in to neither party. If he had done so, he says, "this city would have been widowed of many men. That is why I set myself on defense in both directions and turned at bay like a wolf among many hounds." [28] All this is in iambic trimeters.

In another utterance from an iambic poem Solon says that if somebody else had been given his assignment "he would not have restrained or stopped the people, until by shaking things up he had separated the milk from the butter. *I* set myself as the dividing line in the mid-space between the two hosts." [29] Even more striking is the following, from a poem in trochaic tetrameters. Solon sums up in one imagined speech the ironic judgment of some one of his fellow citizens on his failure to make himself tyrant, master of Athens, when he had the chance: "Solon was not blessed with deep wits and shrewd counsel. God offered him good things, but he would not take them. After he had cast and caught his fish, in his wonder and delight he didn't pull in his big net. He missed, for lack of courage and good sense. If *I* had had the power, had gotten boundless wealth and been Lord of Athens for just one day, I would have been willing to be skinned alive later and let my family be wiped out forever." [30]

Aside from the homeliness and vividness of Solon's images, what strikes one most forcibly in these lines—written perhaps as late as the 570's or even the 560's—is the scope and power of his dramatic imagination. He understands the viewpoint of his critic, he crawls into the fellow's limited soul and talks of fish lost and nets not pulled in, of letting himself be flayed alive if only he could have been tyrant for a day. More impressive still, *Solon sees himself in the round, in the fulness of his historical mission.* The word "I" abounds in these late poems, but not from vanity. The wolf at bay, the dividing marker between the front lines, the protector who held his shield over both parties: he sees himself as he was when he faced his great task, but also as both parties and the rest of the world saw him. Such self-consciousness, such clarity and objectiveness in envisioning one-self together with "the others," is unique among the poets of archaic Greece.[31] Archilochus has a suggestion of it at times, in his self-presentations: "I am the servant of the Lord God of battles, but I also understand the lovely gift of the Muses," and "With the spear my loaf is kneaded, in the spear is my Ismaric wine, on the spear I lean as I drink it,"[32] or again in another way when he sees himself in relationship to the mysterious "rhythm" of events.[33] Sappho too has her moments of objective insight, when she can register her own throbbing temples, veins on fire, and buzzing ears with clinical precision. All the Greek lyric poets are in one way or another discoverers and proclaimers of the self. But they made this discovery, almost all of them, as private or semiprivate persons and as a result of personal grief or thwarted passion. It was through pain, not by taking thought, that the self was discovered in archaic Greece.[34]

That is not Solon's manner. He places himself before us as a public person, and the way to his self-revelation was not through passion but through rational insight into men's characters and motives—other men's as well as his own. Solon sees himself and the others as actors in a single drama, persons involved equally, each according to his lights, in a reciprocal struggle of aims and desires, hopes and values. The unregulated play of individual ego's has been fitted into a larger frame, the structure of Justice, which allows each man his say but assigns him the place and role he deserves: "to each what is owing him." There is now a measure by which to judge the anarchically competing selves, while leaving them all the rich variety of their disparate natures.

This is one entrance portal to the world of tragedy. Tragedy displays to us a rich variety of disparate natures, by preference high-spirited and willful ones, embarked on courses which lead to tragic ends. But for tragedy it is not enough that these be great, colorful personages of long ago, struggling against their adversaries or their stars. They must be brought "home" to us.

And for this reason they are not simply displayed, they present themselves, with all their passions, purposes, justifications, and follies about them. The presentation cannot be from the outside only, for then their fate would never truly come close to us. But neither can it be from the inside only, for they are in loving or hostile contact with others in the play and, always and irreducibly, with the chorus. Thus at a minimum the tragedian must convey to us the hero's perception of himself, as an Achilles nursing his just wrath or an Orestes facing up to his obligation, *and* the chorus's perception of him as a hero or a rebel. Perceptions and evaluations are of the essence in this matter.

The reader may say at this point that I am anticipating by a century: that all this may apply to Sophocles but not to the "primitive" tragedy of Thespis. But that cannot be true. Greek tragedy, by the peculiarity of its form, is committed to a special kind of double vision: the hero's view of himself and the chorus's view of him. The duality belongs to the form and cannot be argued away. The hero is the fulcrum of the whole. Without him there would be no tragedy, or none worth having. But without the chorus there would not be any tragedy either; the hero would be suspended in a vacuum with no sounding board to respond to his passion and no separate standard by which to measure him. Thus the original form of tragedy—single actor and chorus—established a tension which is of its essence.

The fact is that the "primitive" form of Greek tragedy has implicit in it a high sophistication. To all appearance it is a hybrid form: an "actor" from one realm, representing a hero, and a chorus from another, representing "citizens" or "ordinary men" or "the world." It is a commonplace to say that the hero stems directly or indirectly from the epic, and the chorus from lyric poetry. But in order to meet at all—as it is, they remain perilously tangential to each other throughout the life of Greek tragedy—these two worlds had to pass through the eye of a needle. Somehow the two systems or modes of life, that of the hero and that of the chorus, had to be brought to a common focus so that the spectator could take them in together; for if the rays did not meet in his eye they would never meet anywhere. One key to this meeting is Solon's awareness of himself in relation to others who are not himself; more concretely, his awareness of himself as hero, fighting for his honor and his ideal, in relation to others who are not heroes. The tragic hero could not simply step out of the epic frame, bringing his speeches with him; he had to speak a language to which the men of the sixth century could respond in living terms because it conveyed *their* sense of the heroic person surrounded by a real world. It was Solon—little though he knew it or, perhaps, would have approved of it—who made this possible.[35]

The late iambic and trochaic poems show Solon at the farthest reach of his personal Odyssey: most the responsible public servant giving account of his stewardship, and at the same time most the individual identifying himself in relation to other individuals. We have no comparable self-revelation again until Plato—though we can perhaps sense a similar blend of personality and accomplishment in Pericles.

Why did Solon choose iambic and trochaic verses for his final accounting? Must he not have felt that elegiacs were inadequate for such intimate grapplings with reality? He kept them for certain kinds of utterance, for example his warnings against tyranny, but they were too distant and impersonal to express the truth about himself as he had come to see it. For that he needed the directness, the flash and cutting edge of Archilochus' meters. And he wielded Archilochus' instrument with crackling vigor, yet with a seriousness of purpose, a public sense of involvement and responsibility, which is un-Archilochian. It is the high seriousness of heroic combat tempered by Solon's down-to-earth Athenian realism and cast in the form of a direct self-presentation before the Athenian people.

I have dwelt on Solon's poetic testament at some length. We are trying here to find the roots of a sixth-century Athenian phenomenon, tragedy, and we have to accept the fact that So-

Ion is the only poet of sixth-century Athens outside the tragedians themselves. But not only that. There is a suggestion of
tragedy about Solon's later poems. His defense of his own work,
making clear how and why he had resisted the temptation to
become a tyrant himself, went hand in hand with repeated
warnings against the coming tyranny of Pisistratus—in vain.
The narratives of Aristotle, Plutarch, and Diogenes Laertius[36]
reveal a breakdown of communication between Solon and his
people near the end of his life. When he died he must have
seemed a heroic failure, just in proportion as he was the hero
who had saved Athens from civil war and had justified his own
deeds in poetry of a new high seriousness and directness.

   We have left to the last another aspect of Solon's work which
is as germane to our theme as the rest: the introduction of the
Homeric poems into Attica. It is natural to suppose that the
wandering epic bards and rhapsodes included Attica in their
tours, and recently it has been suggested with some plausibility
that Athens was an important way station on the original route
of transmission of the epic from the Mycenaean centers—Mycenae, and above all Pylos— to Ionia.[37] On the other hand, in
our sparse records of bardic and rhapsodic activity before Solon,
for example in the traditions about the wanderings of Homer
and the Homeridae, other place names turn up in abundance
—Chios, the Troad, Smyrna, Miletus, Ios, Delos, Chalkis,
Thebes, Delphi; Athens seldom. No rhapsode is recorded as
having been born in Attica. From the overt evidence, Athens
before Solon appears to be a literary desert. And the same thing
is true in art, so far as Homer is concerned. Aside from two
representations, one on the big Eleusis amphora showing the
blinding of Polyphemus and the other on the "Ram Jug" showing the escape of Odysseus from the Cyclops' cave, little or
nothing is to be found on proto-Attic vases that deals with epic,
particularly with Homeric, themes. Such representations begin
with Sophilus somewhere around 580 and increase markedly
after 570.[38] It has been argued[39] that this swelling stream of

Homer-inspired art stems from the institution of the rhapsodes' contest at the Panathenaic festival, traditionally dated (Eusebius) to 566. According to two ancient authorities the contest was established by Solon himself, according to another by Pisistratus' son Hipparchus.[40]

Whoever its author, the inauguration of the contest at the Panathenaea was a milestone. Here the rhapsodes were constrained to recite in order from a written text, each delivering an assigned section of the poem, and we are told that the competition was restricted to the *Iliad* and the *Odyssey*. A Homeric text—essentially the one that has come down to us[41]—and the beginnings of a Homeric orthodoxy are established here. The contest seals the death warrant of the ancient art of oral epic composition by prescribing a fixed text and by choosing for recitation just two poems, which are thereby set above all others as the "best." But the old art was in decline anyhow,[42] and by way of return for hastening its demise the contest established the solid base of all Attic literature to come; for that literature remains close to Homer and is based from beginning to end on firm expectation of love of the poet and close knowledge of his text by the whole Athenian people. We have no record of such an educational enterprise anywhere else in archaic Greece. From being a culture-poor, backward land, Attica suddenly became *the* repository of the Homeric heritage. It is a commonplace that Homer turned out to be the teacher of all Greeks. Whether we think that that was his own intention or not, we cannot fail to recognize that the initiator of the rhapsodes' contest at Athens had an educational purpose in mind, and one that embraced a whole people.

It may have been Solon who instituted the contest. It may have been Hipparchus, working in his father's name or in his spirit; it may even have been Pisistratus himself. In any case, like the establishment of Homer as the "core curriculum" in the schools, it is in the spirit of Solon. Every word he wrote on his archonship and the crisis in the Athenian state reveals his awareness that the basic problem he faced was intellectual, moral, and spiritual: not simply to alleviate economic misery or achieve a workable political compromise, but to bring both factions—that is, the whole Athenian people—to a true understanding of what constituted the health of a polity. The freedom and unity of Athens, to which Solon devoted the best years and energies of his life, had to be a moral and spiritual unity. And where was the material to be found for this educational task? Not all of it was in Homer—Solon himself also owed much to Hesiod, for example—but there was more of it, and more essential parts of it, there than anywhere else. Courage, tenacity, faithfulness, courtesy and consideration, above all the dedication of one's whole being, up to and including life itself, to an overriding ideal of nobility, *to kalon,* and excellence, *aretê:* this was what Homer had to teach; [43] and such a dedication to something higher than oneself, combined with a belief in the justice of Zeus and a sense of one's obligations to the community, was what Athens must have to survive as a free polity.

Pisistratus, like Solon, had a profound influence on the development of Athens in every field: political, economic, religious, artistic, literary. Unlike Solon, however, he was neither a thinker nor a writer but an organizer, builder, and administrator of genius. Pisistratus began as an ambitious politician and general, a man on horseback, the leader of a faction. He became, not all at once but well before his death, the benevolent despot and fosterer of all Athenian interests. Strengthening Athens' position in the shifting world of diplomacy; building up her agriculture and foreign trade; fostering and consolidating the established cults—of The Twelve Gods, of Olympian Zeus, of Demeter at Eleusis, of Artemis at Brauron—and sponsoring the importation and naturalization of others, notably the Dionysus of Eleutherae, just across the Boeotian border; [44] initiating grandiose architectural projects—the new Telesterion at Eleusis, the "old" temple of Athena (the so-called Hecatompedon) on the Acropolis, the gigantic temple of Olympian Zeus—; fostering the other arts on an equally grand scale, for example vase-making and vase-painting, to such effect that Attic pots and jars came to be known and prized from Gaul to Scythia: in all these areas of constructive activity the great monarch put every other Greek tyrant in the shade.

In the field of literary patronage it is noteworthy that Pisistratus did not do what his sons later did: import distinguished poets from abroad and group them around him as a literary coterie. Pisistratus' patronage of literature, like his other enterprises, had one dominating purpose—aside, of course, from the useful one of glorifying himself. It was dedicated, in sum, to the greatness and prosperity of Athens and Attica as a whole, rather than to the benefit of any single group or faction. That was certainly the purpose of the two great festivals which he founded and developed, the Panathenaea and the Greater or City Dionysia. If Pisistratus did not actually found the Panathenaea, it was undoubtedly he who gave it splendor and international fame; and the new Dionysia was entirely his doing, his most enduring monument. Established in or very close to 534 B.C. to celebrate the common man's god, Dionysus, it was intended even more clearly than the Panathenaea for the whole Athenian people. And from the beginning of the Dionysia tragedy was its central, special feature. Later a series of other "events" were added: dithyrambic contests, satyr-plays, comedy. At the beginning, when Thespis first officially competed, very little of all that was on display. A procession to bring the cult-statue of Dionysus Eleuthereus from its repository outside Athens into the theater, a sacrifice and song, possibly some informal mummings (the "kômoi"): that was all, except for tragedy.[45]

Tragedy was the great innovation at the Dionysia, the new thing that distinguished it from all other festivals, of Dionysus or any other god, in the Greek world. Is it too much to suggest that if tragedy was not created for the Dionysia, the Dionysia was created for it: that Pisistratus established his new festival as a frame for a new kind of poetry which he thought deserved such a setting? Under the usual conception of the growth of tragedy this would hardly be credible. According to that view tragedy was a crude, popular affair in 534 B.C., perhaps with some vestiges of primitive buffoonery still clinging to it: a minor sort of choral performance, interrupted from time to time by colloquies with an "actor" who perhaps still represented Dionysus or some hero connected with his story. It is hard to imagine why the enlightened tyrant should have chosen such a performance to be the head and forefront of his new festival. In the next chapter we shall consider where tragedy could have come from and what it must have been on that day when Pisistratus gave it its permanent institutional setting.

III. Thespis: The Creation
of *Tragôidia*

THE CRUX of our problem is marked by the name of Thespis, to whom we now come.

Unlike Solon and Pisistratus, Thespis can never be more than a name to us. The earliest extant mention of him—if it is indeed he—is in Aristophanes' *Wasps* in 421 B.C.[1] There is no proof or even likelihood that copies of his plays still existed in Aristophanes' time, much less in the fourth century, and therefore no likelihood that Aristotle or his pupils could have used them as sources.[2] The various other remarks about him from antiquity (carefully collected and discussed by Pickard-Cambridge in *Dithyramb Tragedy and Comedy*, pp. 97–121) give us very little solid evidence, and most of that little goes back to Aristotle but no farther.

There is in the first place a question about his name. 'Thespis' looks like one of the "short names" which were popular in Attica: for example Telon (for Telemachus), Admon (for Admetus), Parmis (for Parmenon), Zeuxis (for Zeuxippus).[3] If so, it must be short for *thespesios*, 'divine, divinely speaking,' or possibly for *thespiôidos*, 'divinely singing': in either case a name which it is hard to imagine being given to an Athenian boy in the ordinary course of events. Another and more interesting possibility exists. Twice in the *Odyssey*, at 1. 328 and 8. 498, we find the phrase *thespin aoidên* (nominative case *thespis aoidê*), 'divine song,' referring to the singing of Demodocus and Phemius respectively; and at 17. 385 Phemius himself is called *thespin aoidon* (nominative *thespis aoidos*), 'divine singer.'

Although these facts have been noticed, and the conjecture

put forward that Thespis' name was somehow derived from the *Odyssey* passages, it does not appear that the problem has been taken very seriously. It is not just a question of whether 'Thespis' was Thespis' "real name." What is significant is the possible link with the epic tradition, and more particularly with the tradition of epic recitation. I assume that in sixth-century Athens *aoidos* would have meant first and foremost an *epic* singer, a 'bard,' and that an Athenian of that day, especially after the regular recitations of the whole *Odyssey* had begun (at the Panathenaea), would not have heard the word *thespis* without mentally associating *aoidê* or *aoidos* with it. I therefore propose seriously two alternative hypotheses: (1) that 'Thespis' was indeed our man's real name, given him at birth, or (2) that it was a nickname or epithet given to him or taken by him at some later time. In the first case I should think it a likely further supposition that Thespis' father was himself an *aoidos,* and gave his son the name either in reference to his own singing or by way of prophecy of the son's achievements.[4] Under the second hypothesis the epithet, whether assumed by Thespis himself or conferred on him by others, would still have been meant to connote some 'bardic' achievement, either in epic recitation or in some activity comparable to it. With our lack of further evidence it would be hard if not impossible to choose between these two hypotheses,[5] and I cannot see that it is necessary for our purpose. The basic inference seems to me highly probable, that Thespis had something to do, either by inheritance or through his own activity, with the profession of epic song.

A word also as to Thespis' home in Attica. The Suda, in the biographical article under his name, gives it as Icarios (in northern Attica, near Marathon; also called Icaria). This is the only explicit statement. It does not carry decisive weight, and is offset by another in Clement of Alexandria[6] which calls Thespis simply "Athenian." Athenaeus, in a passage already cited,[7] alleges that both tragedy and comedy were born at Icarios at the time of the vintage festival, and if one holds to Thespis as the inventor one might infer that he was an Icarian. But even this inference is not necessary—Athenaeus only says the event took place at Icarios—and the passage of Clement just mentioned makes Thespis an Athenian while calling Susarion, the alleged inventor of *comedy,* an Icarian. The fact of the matter appears to be that while reliable tradition spoke of Thespis simply as an Athenian, efforts were made in the course of the literary war (mentioned previously, in chapter I[8]), or thereafter, to attach his name to Icarios.[9] Whatever the truth may be about the details, the issue involved is clear: the association with Icarios was a way of connecting him with Dionysus.[10] Otherwise the tradition about Thespis, as we have emphasized before, shows no connection with Dionysus, the dithyramb, or anything Dionysiac. I think we may consider "Thespis the Icarian" another Dionysiac gambit in the game of claims and counterclaims.

Now, what did Thespis do? The explicit testimony from antiquity that has anything of value to tell us can be reduced to two, possibly three, items. Thespis is not mentioned in the extant part of the *Poetics,* but he was in the lost work—probably the lost dialogue *On Poets*—from which Themistius quotes: [11] "Aristotle says that at first the chorus as it came in used to sing to the gods, but Thespis invented a prologue and a (set) speech." [12] Second, the statement of the Parian Marble that the first tragic contest took place in or very close to 534 B.C. is accepted, so far as I know, by all competent judges. The Marble identifies the contest as taking place at the City Dionysia, and our fifth-century evidence makes it certain that that festival was the original home of tragedy. Third and last, Aristophanes in the *Wasps* makes a character speak of "those old-fashioned dances with which Thespis used to compete"; and this Thespis may be, though as we have seen he is not certainly, the tragedian.[13]

That is all we know about Thespis by testimony early enough and solid enough to claim our respect. The statements of others

—Dioscorides in the Greek Anthology, Horace, Athenaeus, *et al.*—are too late or too dubious, or both, to count. Here, then, conjecture and inference necessarily begin. The most important single clue is Aristotle's remark that Thespis invented a prologue and a set speech, a *rhêsis*. These two elements represent between them the dialogue or spoken portion of tragedy, and no responsible scholar doubts, so far as I am aware, that that was Thespis' contribution to the art. The question is, what did it amount to? I mean by this, did tragedy begin with the invention of a spoken part or was that simply a further step in the development of a genre that was already in existence?

We have already dealt with this question from one point of view in the first chapter, but it is so crucial that we must consider it again—and must take great care in answering it. All the principal theories now in the field agree on the second alternative. That is, they assume that tragedy in some sense was already there and Thespis did or added something to it. On what he did and how he did it there is less agreement. According to the standard view, which as we have seen was probably that of Aristotle, Thespis' addition of a speaker simply developed a potentially dramatic element which was already present in the lyrical form of "tragedy." This element would have been represented originally by the *exarchôn* or "leader-off" of the improvised dithyramb, and perhaps later by the *coryphaeus* or chorus leader. Whichever it was, Thespis converted him into an actor by separating him more distinctly from the chorus and giving him set lines to speak. Wilamowitz rejected this interpretation.[14] His chief reason was that the spoken part as we find it in Phrynichus and Aeschylus is too different from the choral part in language and style to be an outgrowth from it. The choral odes have a thin but, on the whole, uniform Doric coloring (chiefly long *a* in place of long *e*); the dialogue, on the other hand, is basically in Attic dialect, though with some Homeric and Ionic infusions. Moreover Wilamowitz pointed out, and Aurelio Peretti later showed in detail,[15] that the structure of the tragic *rhêsis* in the earliest plays of Aeschylus has nothing in common with choral lyric but goes back to Ionian models: epic, elegiac, and iambic poetry.

It is a question whether Wilamowitz assessed correctly the differences in language between dialogue and lyrical parts. In any case the Doric coloring of the odes presents a problem which we will examine later in this chapter.[16] Meanwhile, although Wilamowitz denied that the spoken part could have developed out of the choral and insisted that it must have been added to it from outside, he too held fast to the previous existence of "tragedy," that is, *tragôidia,* the song of goats; so that Thespis' achievement still consisted merely in adding something to an already existing genre. This reduction of Thespis' act to a revision or adaptation of an existing form, and of the actor's part to an appendage, only destined to become the dominant element at a later stage, is not justified by the evidence if one takes all the evidence into account. I believe it can be shown that Thespis created a new genre, instead of merely tinkering with an old one, and that the actor's part and the choral part never existed independently but were invented together, with and for each other. This is a radical thesis, and to prove it or even make it plausible we shall have to marshal several independent lines of argument.

There is one such argument which seems to me decisive in itself, but it is a technical one and needs to be supplemented by other, broader considerations. Since I have presented it elsewhere, in my article on "The Origin of ΤΡΑΓΩΙΔΙΑ,"[17] and have nothing important to add to that presentation, I shall merely summarize it here. We saw in the first chapter that both the etymology *tragôidia* = 'song of goats' and the historical development to which it commits us are impossible. *Tragôidia,* as we said there, is not a simple compound of *tragos,* 'goat,' and *ôidia,* 'song,' but a secondary compound formed from the primary compound *tragôidos,* 'goat-singer.' Thus the beginning of the development must be sought in *tragôidos* rather than in *tragôidia*. And there is good reason to believe that 'goat-singer' referred originally to the poet-actor, the reciter of spoken verses, rather than to the chorus.

We have in a fourth- and third-century inscription, named by Wilamowitz the 'Fasti,' fragments of a complete, year-by-year record of the dramatic and other contests at the Dionysia from the time when they were reorganized at the end of the sixth century.[18] The record perhaps began originally with the year 509/508, more likely with 502/501. In it the word *tragôidoi* (plural) appears in two places, first in the heading at the top and again, this time in the genitive plural *tragôidôn,* as a sub-heading introducing the names of the winners of the tragic contest in each year. It is an easy—I would say a necessary—inference that *tragôidoi* was the official title of the contestants in tragedy, those who actually competed for the prize. But these contestants were just two in number: the so-called *chorêgos* or "chorus-leader" (actually the citizen who paid the costs of the production) and the poet, under the designation *didaskalos,* "teacher" or "trainer" (of the chorus). The tragic chorus itself was not a competitor and won no prize. Furthermore the *chorêgos,* in the special sense used here, certainly does not antedate the introduction of the choregic system, which we can place in one of the same years already mentioned, 509/508 or more likely 502/501. It follows that the original competitor in the tragic contest, and therefore the sole possessor of the title *tragôidos* before the year 509 or 502, was the tragic poet. And the poet was also his own actor; that was the role in which he actually appeared before the public, the conspicuous way in which he competed for the prize.

If this argument is correct, its importance is great. We have already said that the word *tragôidia* was made from *tragôidos.* But if the poet was the original and only *tragôidos,* then *tragôidia* did not originally denote an activity of the chorus, it did not refer directly to the chorus at all, but to the activity of the poet, that is, the poet-actor, or—derivatively—to the total performance of which he was the leading feature. Further, since Thespis was the first tragic poet to appear at the Dionysia he was the first *tragôidos,* and *tragôidia* was what he invented, the performance in which he took the leading role.

Technical arguments like the one just summarized will not carry us all the way. Also, the more logically or geometrically a literary proposition is demonstrated, the less many people are inclined to trust it. This attitude is not unreasonable; and anyhow there is more to be said. If Thespis *was* the first *tragôidos* and the inventor of *tragôidia,* what does this mean? What was it that he invented?

Here another danger faces us, one that has been mentioned before: the assumption that if Thespis invented 'tragedy' he must have invented the tragic *drama.* The farther we go back in the work of Aeschylus, and in the work of his older contemporary Phrynichus so far as we can penetrate it, the less overt drama we find. I take it that close to the heart of drama as we usually conceive it (see the Introduction, page 5) is conflict of some kind between persons; and such conflict is at best marginal or intermittent in Aeschylus, except in his last two plays. Even Agamemnon and Clytemnestra do not quite meet in real conflict; they pass by each other in a curiously sidelong fashion. Eteocles and Polynices do not meet at all on stage; indeed the absence of such an encounter is one of the most striking features of the *Seven against Thebes.* Except for the meeting of the King and the Egyptian Herald in the *Suppliants,* it is notable that Aeschylus does not use his first two actors to stage a conflict. Indeed in the two-actor stage, represented by *Persians, Seven,* and *Suppliants,* the second actor does not normally represent a person who *could* conflict with the hero at all.

If the two-actor form permits no conflict (and in this respect there is not likely to have been any difference between Phrynichus and Aeschylus), what of the one-actor form that preceded it? It is sufficiently clear from the sparse evidence that it was Aeschylus who introduced the second actor. Thespis had only one: himself. What did he do with himself? It has always seemed to me that scholars have pondered this question too little. For at least a full generation, from the 530's to the end of the sixth century, a period during which tragedy obviously flourished and established itself as a major genre, it had just one actor.

The easy answer is that the chorus was in effect a second actor. But this answer will not do. No ordinary group or representative of a group, like the chorus-leader, can take the part of an individual and conflict or even debate on equal terms with the hero.[19] The chorus' collective character is fatal to drama—unless the poet can find a particular situation for it that is dramatic. And anyhow the chorus of Greek tragedy is almost invariably composed of persons below the social and moral level of the hero. The choruses of *Suppliants* and *Eumenides* are notable exceptions. I hope to show later that they are brilliantly and peculiarly Aeschylean innovations. We must not be misled by the false early dating of the *Suppliants* into thinking of the chorus as the protagonist in primitive tragedy. The chorus as protagonist is a sophisticated development, prompted by specific motives which we shall explore in the next chapter.

The Thespian actor was alone, then. That is not to say that he did not converse or communicate with the chorus. But this kind of conversation is not proved, as many have assumed, by the Greek term for 'actor,' *hypokritês*.[20] The original meaning of *hypokritês* has been much discussed of late. Usually it is thought to mean 'answerer,' but recently several scholars have come round to the signification 'explainer, interpreter.' I believe that this view is wrong and the old, standard one is correct, that *hypokritês* means basically 'answerer.' But this does not prove that Thespis was called a *hypokritês* or that the first *hypokritês,* whoever he was, was so denominated because he answered the chorus. In the latter part of the fifth century the tragic actors, all of them, were called *hypokritai*. But down at least through Aeschylus—perhaps Sophocles also, in his early years—the poets were their own leading actors, and I have argued elsewhere and still maintain that at that time they were called *tragôidoi*.[21] If so, they cannot also have been called *hypokritai*. Instead I would maintain that the term was first applied to those actors who were only actors and not *tragôidoi*—as we would say, the second and third actors. Later, when the poets gave up acting, the term was generalized and extended to cover the whole tragic company. Thespis, then, was a *tragôidos*, not a *hypokritês*.

Leaving etymologies aside, however, neither can Thespis' function as an actor have consisted in answering the chorus. The very text that might seem to confirm this supposition invalidates it. Aristotle says, we recall, "At first the chorus as it came in used to sing to the gods, but Thespis invented a prologue and a *rhêsis*." Neither of these latter terms smacks of conversation, question and answer. But we have more positive evidence to go on than inferences from Aristotle. There are prologues and *rhêseis* in early Aeschylean plays. Here again understanding has been impeded, this time by the fact that the *Suppliants* has no prologue. For that matter neither has the *Persians,* which we now know to be the earliest extant play. But we also know that the *Persians* was written as some kind of counter to the *Phoenician Women* of Phrynichus, produced four years earlier, in 476 B.C., and the *Phoenician Women* did have a prologue.[22] Thus after some years of misapprehension we can again accept the idea that tragedy had a prologue from the time of Thespis, as Aristotle says it did.

What was the content of Thespis' prologues? Were they dramatic, that is, spoken in character, or expository, spoken by the poet in his own person to introduce the play, set forth the background of the story, and ask for a favorable hearing? We cannot say for sure. The parallels in the epic and lyric domain, in the so-called "Homeric hymns," which are really *prooimia* or preludes to epic recitation, and the *proomion* of the Apollinian nome, are not decisive. Yet it seems to me that much the most plausible source for the Thespian prologue—that is, for the idea of a prologue—is the bard's or rhapsode's prelude. The wandering bard needed to introduce himself to the public, announce his theme, and arouse the curiosity and if possible the benevolence of his audience toward his song, or if nothing more, simply to give time for the babble of voices to die down so that he could be heard. Choral poetry had less need of such preliminaries *vis-à-vis* its audience; the group's entrance and taking of position, or the first notes of the flute, would suffice. (Even so it is worth remarking that Pindar and Bacchylides incorporate introductory matter of some kind into most odes, as a way to get started.)—Surely it is no accident that the nome, a solo performance and itself ultimately derived from epic song, is the one lyric genre with a formally marked *prooimion*.

One thing, I think, we can be fairly sure of: the original tragic prologue was not spoken, as it often is in Euripides, by a god. There is no reason to believe that gods appeared on the stage before Aeschylus. It is more likely that Thespis' prologue was simply and frankly introductory. But we cannot exclude the possibility that he appeared in character as the hero of the piece, introducing himself and reminding the audience of the background of his story.

With the other innovation which Aristotle ascribes to Thespis, the *rhêsis* or set speech, we are on firmer ground. The earlier plays of Aeschylus abound in *rhêseis*. Peretti has studied their structure, their *êthos,* and their function in the play and shown[23] that they have three marked traits in common: (1) a rather strict tripartite structure ("ring composition"), such that the thought enunciated at the beginning of the speech is restated at the end, after an intermediate section of development; (2) an objective mode of presentation, dry and logical rather than lyrical in spirit; and (3) a decisive effect of the *rhêsis* upon the following scene: that is, the *rhêsis* determines or sets in motion what follows, including usually the next song of the chorus. Almost always the content of the *rhêsis* is either a *parainesis,* an exhortation to action, or a description of a state of affairs which is thus brought before the hearer and elicits a response from the chorus. In other words the actor's *rhêsis* and the reaction of the chorus appear in that order, as cause and effect. The actor determines and shapes the participation of the chorus, not the other way round. The chorus appears throughout as the passive, the receiving partner.

Peretti's analysis, including a comparison with later plays of Aeschylus, leaves no doubt that these features of the older Aeschylean *rhêseis* are survivals from an earlier stage of tragedy. "Ring-composition" especially is a well-known archaic mode. The formal ties with elegy and elegiac *parainesis* are particularly close. On the other hand the tragic *rhêseis* are not in elegiac couplets but in trochaic tetrameters or iambic trimeters, mainly the latter. The use of these meters has to be explained. Actually they are one of our most important clues to the original form and spirit of tragedy.

Aristotle says in the *Poetics* (4.1449a21 ff.) that trochaic tetrameter was the original verse of tragedy because trochaics are a dance rhythm and early tragedy was mainly a dance performance. "Then," he says, "when speech [as opposed to song] put in an appearance, the meter changed to iambic trimeter"—because, he adds, iambic is the natural rhythm of speech, dialogue. Rightly interpreted, Aristotle's remark does not refer to Aeschylus or even to Sophocles, as it has been thought to do, but to Thespis; for it was Thespis, according to Aristotle himself, who introduced speech into tragedy. In any case the spoken verses in the earlier extant plays are in fact overwhelmingly iambic; trochaic tetrameters figure importantly only in the *Persians,* and then not as a dance meter. There are no hexameters or elegiac couplets. And this limitation must go back to Thespis: we know of no one after him who could have enforced it. Iambic is the chosen medium of tragic dialogue.

'Iambic,' as a class, embraces iambics, usually in the form of iambic trimeters, and trochaics, usually in the form of tetrameters. In the ancient tradition iambic poetry figures as the invention of Archilochus, and it was always considered to have a special *êthos* or character: sharp, vituperative, satirical. This recognized *êthos* of iambic constitutes a problem. Why did tragedy, of all literary genres, choose the particular verse form that was identified with satire, vilification, the uninhibited expression of personal hatreds and animosities? Thespis cannot have adopted it for such a reason. We have to assume another use of iambic which was quite different from that of Archilochus, yet so significant and impressive that Thespis felt impelled to use it for his new purpose. Once the problem is put this way, the answer is clear. There is only one possible model: those iambic and trochaic poems of Solon which we discussed in the last chapter. Solon had chosen these verse forms, in preference to the elegiac couplet, as the appropriate vehicle for that *parainesis* or exhortation of his fellow citizens which was also his ripest and most direct self-revelation. If Thespis adopted them from Solon, it must have been for a similar reason. But in that case what idea was it that he wanted to convey, that could be carried better by iambics than by hexameters or elegiac couplets?

Here, by way of the verse form, we begin to approach the heart of the matter, the inner content and purpose of Thespis' new creation. But we cannot assay that content and purpose until we have considered another large aspect of the question: the tragic myth. On this subject a great deal of nonsense has been spread abroad in the last fifty years. Thanks in part to the ancient theories of an origin out of dithyramb and/or satyr-play, in part to modern developments in anthropology, psychology, etc., the concepts of *myth* and *ritual* have got tangled up together in well-nigh hopeless confusion. So far as tragedy is concerned, one of the ideas to which this has led is that it must have begun as some kind of ritualistic representation of the doings or sufferings of Dionysus (Dionysus broadly or narrowly conceived) but later lost its direction, or simply reached out for other material, and came to deal more and more with other gods and heroes. Or, alternatively, as we saw, a similar connection is postulated with hero-cult, the worship of dead ancestors in various parts of Greece.

Against this modern obsession with myth and ritual, or ritual origins of myth, we must insist on two facts: (1) The content of the overwhelming majority of known tragedies (and we know the titles and/or the content of many more than are now extant) is *heroic* myth or legend, from Homer and the epic Cycle. Affiliations with cult-myths and cult-rituals, especially those of Dionysus, are secondary both in extent and importance.[24] In other words the regular source of tragic material is heroic epic, not religious cult. (2) Above all, the standard tragic myths are not Athenian. As we said before, Attica was poor in myths compared to most of her neighbors on the mainland. Connections of the heroic legend with Attica, either by bringing the hero there—Orestes before the Areopagus, Iphigenia to Brauron, Oedipus to Colonus—or by sending an Athenian abroad—Aegeus to Corinth in the *Medea,* Theseus to Thebes in the *Hercules Furens*—are clearly secondary, as is the development of purely Attic material (Theseus is the chief example of the latter). There is, moreover, no reason to suppose any change in these respects between Thespis and Aeschylus. The conclusion is obvious: tragedy did not begin as cult-drama, Dionysiac or otherwise, and its mythical material normally had nothing to do with Athens.

How are we to explain this paradox, that the most uniquely Attic genre began with non-Attic content? The answer cannot be given in full detail and with complete confidence, because we are dealing with a creative act which can only be approached tentatively and indirectly (creativity is not fully explainable even if one knew all the external facts). Thespis' creative act was to express epic content, drawn from heroic myth, in Solonian form (iambic verses) combined with choral songs. In my article on "The Origin of ΤΡΑΓΩΙΔΙΑ" I suggested that tragedy grew out of the rhapsodes' recitations of Homer, and I connected the event with the fact, already mentioned here, that Athens was the one place in Greece in the sixth century where Homer was recited regularly and in full to the whole people. This formulation is still valid, I believe, but it needs to be qualified and extended.

The mysterious event we are trying to apprehend can perhaps be characterized provisionally this way: Thespis felt in Homer the compelling reality of the heroic nature and the heroic fate; he wanted to give this vision and feeling some immediate expression, more direct and pungent than it received in the recitations of Homer; and finally, something in Solon's use of iambic and trochaic verse suggested to him that this was the appropriate medium. Thespis' new creation, therefore, brought together three different things which had never been joined before: the *epic hero, impersonation,* and *iambic verse*.[25] The hero is the subject; he presents himself directly, in his own character, instead of through quasi-impersonation by the rhapsode; and he speaks in iambics and trochaics instead of hexameters. Each of these elements calls for some further elucidation before we can understand what it was that Thespis produced by combining them.

First, the epic hero; not the epic as such. Greek tragedy was never at any stage of its development simply a dramatization of epic narrative. (We may contrast Shakespeare, who often dramatized narrative material, historical or fictional.) It concentrates upon a few incidents, even a single incident, in the hero's career. I suggest that this concentration, which has always been remarked by judicious critics, must have been a feature of tragedy from its birth. In Aeschylus, and especially in the early works, it goes so far that hardly anything happens in the play at all. In the *Persians,* strictly speaking, nothing happens; the disaster is over before the play begins. In the *Seven against Thebes* Eteocles mans the gates, fights his brother, and dies; that is all, and none of these events actually takes place on stage. Moreover both these plays center upon a single hero. Eteocles' isolation is an essential, not an accidental, part of his situation. The epic scene is crowded with heroes; the oldest tragedies present a single one.

We are entitled to extrapolate from these facts, to argue back from them to the form and spirit of Thespian tragedy. Tragedy did not begin as a transposition of epic material into dramatic form, complete with debate, conflict, battle; it began as a self-presentation of a single epic hero. Not of the hero's actions; that comes later. And not simply of the hero himself either, as a person: a study of his character or his thoughts and feelings. But it was a self-presentation none the less, of the hero's *situation,* his fate. And this situation has a special focus: not what the hero does but what he suffers; not his display of prowess, his moment of glory on the battlefield or in council, but his moment of disaster or failure: death, loss, humiliation. I propose to call this moment the hero's *pathos*: borrowing a term from the *Poetics*[26] but giving it a somewhat wider extension than Aristotle does. And I propose a further thesis, one of the most important in this book: that the whole development of Greek tragedy, from the beginning to the end of its life span, was a flowering from this single root, the hero's *pathos*. (Perhaps one corollary might be pointed out at once. It is often said that Greek tragedy, unlike later tragedy, was not always tragic. That is partly true, partly false. Greek tragedies do not always end tragically; but their root is always a tragic situation.)

Why did Thespis choose the *pathos* as his center? Because for some reason it was what impressed him most about the hero, spoke most directly to his sensibility. Not the hero's life but his death, not his success but his failure, not the superhuman valor and might which set him off from the rest of us who eat the bread of earth, but that which allies him with us: death, mortality, suffering. For the same reason Thespis did not present the hero quite alone. He added another element, the chorus, to be a sounding board for the heroic passion. The chorus is made up of ordinary mortals like us, and through their emotional participation in the hero's fall we too are drawn into the ambit of his *pathos*. The chorus is our link with him.

This link is not an arbitrary one. The tragic hero, whatever his antecedents in myth, is not a demigod. His force and powers may be beyond ours but he is also, as Aristotle says, "like us." He can err and suffer and die, and this human liability to error and suffering and death, combined with his greatness, is what moves the chorus to lament him and moves us to join in the lament. Seldom in Greek tragedy (save perhaps in the *Oedipus at Colonus*) is the stark fact of death softened by any suggestion of survival, and then not in the sense of personal immortality. Except in men's memories and affections there is no life beyond the grave, no assurance of ultimate victory over our human condition.

But the link provided by the chorus is not merely human and generic. Fifth-century tragedy has two kinds of choruses, male and female. Tradition has it, and plausibly, that female roles, both individual and choral, were introduced by Phrynichus.[27] The male choruses of Aeschylus and Sophocles fall into two classes: (1) followers or dependants of the hero, as in Aeschylus' *Myrmidons, Phrygians,* etc., Sophocles' *Ajax* and *Philoctetes;* and (2) citizens, most often elders and councillors of state, as in *Persians* and *Agamemnon, Antigone* and *Oedipus Rex*. These two categories represent groups bound to the hero by special ties: in the one case a feudal, quasi-familial relationship, in the other a civic one. There is no visible reason why both types should not go back to Thespis. The citizen chorus is the root manifestation of the political element in Greek tragedy, an element which distinguishes it clearly from epic. Through it the audience is bound into a special relationship with the hero. In *Agamemnon* the audience becomes a part of the citizen body of Argos; in *Oedipus,* of Thebes. Or, alternatively, these heroes become as if they were Athenians. Thus in mourning the hero the chorus, and through it the audience, is lamenting *its* king or great man and so lamenting in its own cause. The expression of sorrow is a communal act, a shared experience of the whole body politic. I would urge that this was an essential, indeed *the* essential, feature of Thespian tragedy.

Cantarella in his book on Aeschylus[28] points out that the epic tradition, and more specifically the heroic myth, reached a crisis about the middle of the sixth century. By that time the tradition was ancient and venerable and fast becoming the common patrimony of all Greeks, carried to every nook and corner of the nation by the rhapsodes. Yet inwardly it was dying, if not already dead. The epic machinery and conventions, the exploits and postures of the heroes, still commanded respectful, even rapt attention. But they had less and less pertinence to real life. What did the epic have to say to a man, especially a commoner, caught up in the fierce struggle for moneymaking ("money, money [*chrêmata*] is the man," was the motto of the time), economic misery and insecurity, political *stasis* between nobles and commons, religious qualms and religious indifference, the hard battle to earn a living and be a citizen?

What the epic had to say to sixth-century men was something that had lost some of its immediate but none of its ultimate relevance: a message for the mind and heart. It spoke of the heroic spirit, of valor and courtesy and self-respect and devotion to an ideal of conduct; and it spoke of death and suffering. The Homeric ideal of bravery in the face of death had already been caught up and transmitted to the citizen-soldier of the seventh century through the elegies of Callinus and Tyrtaeus. But that was a relatively easy ideal to transmit, it had firmness and grandeur but little spiritual depth; and the times had changed. The Spartan of Tyrtaeus' day, or even later, might be fired by simple exhortations to bravery, honor, self-sacrifice for the fatherland; Archilochus was already deaf to them in the seventh century, as he was to the whole official apparatus of heroism; and in sixth-century Athens they had lost even more of their resonance. The Athenians were no Spartans. For them the Homeric message could be made a reality again only through a new approach, a new, inward apprehension of what it means to be a hero and die a hero. Such an apprehension would have to grasp not only the heroic but the tragic side of the Homeric vision.

Solon was not quite a Homeric hero. He himself was too sober, too concentrated on present reality, perhaps too intellectual (it is not easy for the intellectual man to be a hero or to be taken as one).[29] But Solon was profoundly serious; he struggled hard to realize an ideal greater than himself, and his struggle ended in apparent failure, the negation of what he had worked for. To a sympathetic observer in his later years he might well seem a new Hector who had sacrificed himself in vain for his homeland and the welfare of his people. With this difference: that Solon was conscious of his own historical position, and he was superbly self-expressive. Certainly he was the one Athenian in the sixth century who came nearest to heroic stature, and he was the one who presented himself with the greatest vividness, especially in his iambic and trochaic poems. Was it not, then, from him or through him—from what other figure, living or dead, could it have been?—that Thespis caught the idea of a self-presentation of the hero?

As we said earlier, three things were wrapped up together in Thespis' creation: *self-presentation* of the hero and his *pathos* in *iambic* verses. Idea and form or inner and outer form came together. Probably Thespis could not have separated them, so closely were they identified with each other in his own mind. Theoretically, however, and even historically, we can make a certain disjunction. The use of iambic verse for this kind of purpose could have come to Thespis only from Solon. The other side of his invention, the direct impersonation of a character, had two roots, one in Solon, the other in the recitations of Homer. We referred in the preceding chapter to Solon's impersonation of a herald in the delivery of his own poem "Salamis." That kind of political dramatization was matched and surpassed by Pisistratus, who paved the way to his first tyranny by stage-managing an ambush of which he was the apparent vic-

tim, and who made his second entry into Athens as the new
Odysseus, escorted by a live Athena standing beside him in a
chariot. But back of Solon and Pisistratus stands Homer, the
Homer of the rhapsodes. I have discussed this subject elsewhere[30] and can be brief here. The rhapsodes did not merely recite Homer, they acted him, and from this quasi-impersonation
of Homeric characters it was only a step to full impersonation,
from the rhapsode who momentarily spoke in the person of
Achilles or Odysseus to the "actor" who presented himself as
Achilles or Odysseus.

It has been claimed that dramatic impersonation in Greek
tragedy stems, as it often has elsewhere, from magic and ritual:
that it involves a self-identification of the cult-actor or partici-
pant in cult with his god or demon. This allegation, plausible
as it sounds, is refuted by two stubborn facts that have already
been mentioned: (1) the Greek tragic actor's impersonation is
not normally of gods or demons but of epic heroes, and heroes
who for the most part did not possess a cult in Attica; and (2)
the actor's speeches, as we first glimpse them in Aeschylus, are
not spoken as if by one possessed, but on the contrary in a
sober, rational, even pedantic style, without a trace of frenzy.
Actually, as Cantarella pointed out,[31] the *logos,* the speech or
discourse of the tragic actor, is not only un-dithyrambic and
un-Dionysiac, it is anti-Dionysiac. The tragic hero presents
himself as an irreducibly separate person. His self-awareness is
at the opposite pole from the Dionysiac frenzy of self-abandonment, the drowning of all individuation in a mystical unity.
There is no place in the development of the tragic actor for
Ergriffenheit or "possession," Dionysiac or other.

The genetic connection between epic rhapsode and tragic actor is confirmed, I believe, by the etymological situation. We
have already surveyed that portion of the evidence which suggests that the poet-actor was originally called *tragôidos.* Now
rhapsôidos and *tragôidos* are analogous though not identically
formed compounds. In my article on the origin of *tragôidia*

I proposed an explanation of *rhapsôidos* ('stitch-singer' or 'stitch-bard'), tracing it to the peculiar kind of Homeric recitation from a fixed text which was prescribed at the Panathenaea. But the etymology is not essential to our present argument. Whatever the original meaning and application of *rhapsôidos,* its phonetic shape betrays it as an Attic word. The same is true of *tragôidos,* and I suggest that the latter was modeled on the former.

We have seen how much havoc has been wrought by the idea that *tragôidia* must mean 'song of goats.' *Tragôidos* does not really mean 'goat-singer' either. It is true that the root *aeid-aoid-* (*aeidô, aoidos, -ôidos, aoidê, ôidê*) means 'sing.' But the *aoidoi* or epic bards certainly went over from singing to some form of recitation at some period and yet continued to be called 'singers'; and the *rhapsôidoi* did not sing, they recited. In other words, by the sixth century if not before, the word *aoidos* and the suffix *-ôidos* no longer necessarily denoted actual singing. They were conventional terms: much as we can still call a poet a "singer" if we like, without meaning that he utters musical notes. *Tragôidos* was cut from the same cloth as *rhapsôidos,* and did not mean either that its bearer sang or that he impersonated a goat. What it did mean is sufficiently clear from the Parian Marble, which tells us that the original prize for which the "tragedian" competed was a goat. Very likely the name was ironic when it was first bestowed: "goat-bard" might convey the suggestion.

We have considered the *tragôidos,* and we have suggested two possible types of tragic chorus. What did the chorus actually do? Almost everything is possible except that it was a goat-chorus or that it sang real dithyrambs; for the dithyramb is the one lyric genre of which there is little or no trace in fifth-century lyrics. Otherwise Aeschylus' choruses sing a great variety of songs, and it is possible that Thespis already covered much of this range. At any rate there are two varieties of lyric which we can assign to him with great plausibility: the hymn, and the *thrênos* or lamentation. We recall that according to Aristotle "at first the chorus as it came in used to sing to the gods." More particular evidence is afforded by the plays of Aeschylus, every one of which contains a hymn to Zeus and/or other gods, or at least elements of the hymn. Most often it comes at the beginning, in the *parodos* of the chorus. And the end of the *Persians* and that of the *Seven,* the two oldest extant plays, contain equally clear examples of the *thrênos.* Peretti and Hölzle,[32] following in the footsteps of Martin Nilsson, have shown that these *thrênoi* of tragedy, with their epirrhematic structure (alternation of speech and song), their repetitive cries and refrains, and their passionate spirit of lamentation, are survivals of an older form which had clearly marked features. The dochmiac meter in particular, which appears in tragic *thrênoi* and other passages of similar *êthos,* and which was always restricted to tragedy (neither choral lyric nor comedy uses it), is very probably an Attic-Ionic verse-form traditionally associated with the lamentations for the dead. The lyric iambics of which Aeschylus is so especially fond, and which are often associated with dochmiacs, belong to the same Attic-Ionic sphere.[33]

But at this point we must face a problem which was mentioned earlier in the chapter but postponed.[34] We said there that Wilamowitz had called attention to the difference between the choral parts of fifth-century tragedy, which show a uniform Doric coloring, and the dialogue, which is essentially in Attic dialect, though with some Homeric and Ionic infusions. This difference did not disturb Wilamowitz, since he believed that the dialogue part stemmed from the sphere of Ionic epic and elegy and was merely added externally, juxtaposed, to a choral element (*tragôidia*) derived from Peloponnese. But a theory like the one proposed here, which insists that tragedy was an exclusively Athenian affair in origin, cannot rest content with this solution. If the choral parts do indeed have a uniformly Doric coloring, is not that a sign that they were derived from

Peloponnese after all, as the conventional theory maintains? Unfortunately the question cannot be argued in full here. For one thing the facts are much more complex than our previous brief mention would lead the reader to suppose. Doric words and forms also appear in tragic dialogue. Björck, after a thorough investigation of them, concluded that they represent various special types of borrowing, particularly where no exact Attic equivalent was available.[35] It follows that they are not in very different case from the Homeric and Ionic borrowings. On the other hand, Homericisms and Ionicisms also appear in the choral parts, though in considerably less density.[36] The true fact of the matter appears to be that the basic texture of both parts, dialogue and choral, is Attic, but with Homeric and Ionic influences more prominent in the dialogue and Doric in the choral odes.[37] (One significant feature is that the syntax almost without exception, so far as we can tell, is Attic.)

The language of Attic tragedy in both its subvarieties, sung and spoken, is a *Kunstsprache,* an artificial language never actually spoken by anybody but created or developed for poetic purposes. Thanks to the labors of several generations of scholars we are now tolerably familiar with another such Greek language, the Homeric *Kunstsprache,* and we can see that it, though basically Ionic, is not identical with any actual Ionic dialect of any period.[38] Indeed its most striking trait is its complexity; and this complexity includes a strong admixture of non-Ionic forms. Some scholars would like to trace the language of tragedy, in the choral parts, to an equally developed and well-defined Doric *Kunstsprache,* the language of sixth-century choral melic poetry. But although the tendency towards a Doric choral *koinê* certainly existed, we shall probably never be able to define it with any great precision, because of the sparsity of our material; and what is more important, it almost certainly never attained a fixity and uniformity comparable to that of the Homeric *koinê*—partly because the genre, by its very nature, was originally attached primarily to local occasions, partly because of the great variety of song forms included under it, partly because choral lyric had no internationally recognized and stable professional body of singers comparable to the rhapsodes to give its language stability and permanence.[39]

Thus when we speak of a Doric choral language which was transmitted to or imitated by Attic tragedy we are in danger of ascribing too much consistency and definiteness to what was in fact no more than a general tendency. And when we try to apply the concept to tragedy we are bothered again by the relative sparseness of our material—thirty-two tragedies out of many hundreds, perhaps thousands, that were written in the fifth century—and also by more than a passing suspicion that our tragic texts are not reliable on this very point.[40]

In spite of these limitations and reservations, there is no doubt that the choruses of tragedy have a certain Doric coloring—thin and not highly consistent, but unmistakable. How is it to be explained? When we consider that the choruses show very few Doricisms in diction and word formation which are not repeated or paralleled in the dialogue portions, except the "Doric" long *a* (which for that matter is common to all Greek dialects outside of Attic and Ionic), the most circumspect explanation would seem to be that the *Kunstsprache* of tragedy as a whole has been influenced by the somewhat earlier *Kunstsprache* of Dorian choral lyric, but that the influence is more evident and more extensive in the choral parts, as we should expect it to be.

When the matter is put in this way, the period of the Dorian influence and the channel through which it came are not hard to divine. In the last quarter of the sixth century, possibly a little earlier, the dithyramb was imported into Athens—no doubt chiefly from Corinth, although on that point we have no direct information—and cultivated thereafter with great enthusiasm. The two chief men who are associated with this development in our tradition are Lasos and Simonides.[41] Both were active in the dithyrambic contests: Simonides indeed well into the fifth century, if he could correctly boast around 478 that he had won fifty-six prizes in Athens, and Lasos may actually have been instrumental in setting up the first contests, under the Pisistratids.[42] It would be absurd to suppose that tragedy and dithyramb could have been vigorously cultivated side by side in Athens, at the same festival, for thirty or forty years without influences passing from one to the other. And on the choral side the greater influence would naturally come from the dithyramb, with its international standing and its longer tradition (going back to Arion).[43]

One warning: when we say "dithyramb" here we mean the literary dithyramb as Arion had shaped it, dealing with heroic legend and having hardly any more relevance to Dionysus than we have ascribed to tragedy.

The idea of a *stylistic* influence exerted by the heroic dithyramb upon tragedy *in Athens* during the *last quarter of the sixth century* and the beginning of the fifth, is worlds removed from the traditional derivation of tragedy from the dithyramb, whether in Peloponnese or Athens. The essential thing about tragedy—its form—could never have been derived from the dithyramb or from any lyric genre. The self-presentation of the hero is a new idea. And the tragic chorus likewise is a new thing. Its function and status, its *raison d'être,* can only stem from its relation to the hero. Once created, however, the tragic chorus was a chorus also. It sang songs: hymns, paeans, prosodia, whatever was required. The structure and diction of these songs naturally reflected that of choral lyric. And it sang laments, *thrênoi.* The best witness to the strength of the dithyrambic influence, but also to the vitality and integrity of the tragic form, is the fact that the *thrênoi* of Aeschylean tragedy, though they show the same superficial Doric coloring as the other odes, have preserved their ancient Attic structure and spirit.

Phrynichus must have cultivated the threnetic element with special success. The two plays of his which we know something about, the *Capture of Miletus* and the *Phoenician Women,* would appear to have been little more than long-drawn-out

thrênoi. And this is in harmony with the tradition that Phrynichus introduced female roles and female choruses; for women
were traditionally the chief carriers of lamentation for the dead.
But the ritual form of the *thrênos* is very old. It and its constituent elements go back far beyond Homer, to the beginnings
of Greek culture, not as a literary form but as a part of life.[44]
There is no reason, therefore, why Thespis could not have transplanted it into tragedy. But here a fundamental distinction is
necessary. As we saw, Nilsson and others, dissatisfied with the
dithyramb-satyr-play theory, wanted to derive tragedy as a
whole from ritual *thrênoi*. But that theory will not work either,
as it stands. The key to the dilemma is that the tragic *thrênos*
is a ritual element introduced into a non-ritual setting and for
a new purpose, to bewail a person who is neither a member of
the family nor an object of worship but a hero of poetry. The
feelings and forms traditionally associated with the cult of
one's own dead are here transferred to a poetic individual, a
figure of the imagination with whom one has no direct ties of
blood or family.

This transference can be connected, I think, with another
reform which is ascribed to Solon in our tradition. The great
Dipylon vases of the Geometric period in Athens (9th and
especially 8th century) were funerary offerings. They show us
the pomp and splendor of funerals in the great Athenian
families: corteges crowded with mourners, lamentations at the
bier, costly offerings. By Solon's time these funerals had become
the occasion for such outrageous displays of family wealth and
pride that he was moved to curtail them drastically.[45] Solon's
motive was not, like the elder Cato's, puritanism. He knew his
Athenians and their love of funerals, but he also saw that funerary display was helping to confirm the self-esteem of the great
families and thus to perpetuate the division between nobles and
commoners. I would not go so far as to suggest that Thespis'
invention of tragedy was part of Solon's reforms or directly
prompted by political motives. We do not even know whether

Thespis instituted his new kind of performance before Solon's death.[46] But its effect was in accord with Solon's purpose.

In a deeper sense I think it can be said that Thespis' invention carried forward the whole work of Solon on a new front. The *Iliad,* with its dual vision of heroism and the tragic limits of heroism, is the root of all tragedy in the Western world, and therefore of all tragedy. But it took Thespis' act of genius to bring the Homeric vision into focus for a new age. The *Iliad* deals only with the heroes; the common man is present only as backdrop, stage setting, or else as the audience, sitting and listening to a far-off tale of long ago. Tragedy for the first time brought the far-away directly into the present and the great man into direct contact with the little man. It did these two things through the twin devices of the 'actor' and the chorus. Through the actor, who *was* the hero standing before him, and the chorus, which was "like himself," the ordinary Athenian was enabled to feel, to sympathize, with the hero in a new, direct way. Here all Athenians, noble and commoner alike, could meet on common ground, in a common surge of emotional identification with the heroic spirit. And all this was done through forms—iambic verse, *rhêsis,* hymn, *thrênos*—which were familiar, a living part of Athenian experience, and therefore sure of their emotional effect. Tragedy represented, in effect, the beginning of a new spiritual unification of Attica.

We cannot venture a sample scenario of a Thespian tragedy. No doubt the plays—if we can call them that—were even shorter than those of Aeschylus. We can be sure that the performance normally began with a prologue, and that its central feature was the self-presentation of an epic hero. There may have been several short scenes or "episodes," each followed by a song of the chorus. The burden of the whole was a *pathos,* the death or suffering of a hero. The chorus entered with a hymn to Zeus and/or other gods; later, normally at the end, it sang a *thrênos* or formal lamentation over the hero. Such, in barest outline, was the earliest form of tragedy.

As before, we have left Pisistratus to the very end. His function, here too, was that of organizer and continuator. His motive for supporting tragedy must have been at least to some extent pedagogical: he wanted tragedy to stand forth as the educator of his people, as Homer did at the Panathenaea. And perhaps we can conjecture that he had an even more specific idea in mind: tragedy, along with Homer, as an instrument for the *rapprochement* of the classes, an emotional unification of all Athenians in a common sympathy for fallen greatness.[47] Whatever his motives, Pisistratus gave tragedy what it most needed for survival after his death: an institutional home and a *modus vivendi*. He established it as the center and crown of his new festival for all Athenians, the Dionysia. The way was now made ready for the eventual coming of the second genius who would transform *tragôidia* into tragic drama.

IV. Aeschylus: The Creation
of Tragic Drama

ANYONE WHO has read or seen the *Agamemnon* knows that Aeschylus was a great dramatic poet. Thespis necessarily remains remote, a little unreal; what we actually see standing across the path that leads to the beginnings of tragedy is the mighty shade of Aeschylus. All that is grand, all that is searching and heart-shaking in the tragic realm seems to begin with him. So obvious is this, indeed, that the title of Gilbert Murray's well known book, *Aeschylus, The Creator of Tragedy* (Oxford 1940), does no more than express a general consensus.

But surely there cannot be two creators of tragedy? The crucial role we have assigned to Thespis might seem to reduce Aeschylus to the level of a continuator and developer of another man's creation. This chapter will try to show that that is not the case; that a creative achievement of the first magnitude was reserved for Aeschylus, an achievement which in no way yields to the work of Thespis either in originality or in significance for the future of tragedy.

We said at the beginning that Thespis and Aeschylus represent not so much two stages in a process of development as two successive acts of creation, the one of *tragôidia,* the other of tragic drama. One would like to know what happened during the generation that elapsed between the first tragic contest in the 530's and the first appearance of Aeschylus in the lists at the beginning of the fifth century.[1] But that period is very thinly covered in our literary record, and actually there is no reason to suppose that if we had more evidence it would change the picture in any essential respect. Aside from minor inventions and modifications ascribed to Phrynichus,[2] there are just two things of moment to be said about tragedy during this dark period, and one of them cannot be more than an unverifiable surmise.

In the years immediately following 510, after the expulsion of the Pisistratids, Athens became a democracy. Clisthenes, the prime mover in this development, appears to have been a man of vigor and imagination, and his work endured; [3] but he was not a Solon. There is no poetry, no call to spiritual or moral regeneration. In any case the young democracy promptly faced severe trials. It had to fight hard against oligarchic neighbors, Thebes, Aegina, Megara, Corinth. Then came the Ionian revolt against the Persian Empire, from 499 to 494, conspicuously encouraged and supported by Athens. Its collapse was followed very shortly by the first invasion of Greece under Darius, in 490, and ten years later by that of Xerxes. Then, at Marathon and at Salamis, Athens suddenly emerged as the moral champion and leader of the Greek nation. It was a peripety for which other Greeks were not prepared and which some of them found hard to accept, then and afterward. But the facts could not be denied. The sheer glory of the charge at Marathon; the heroism with which the Athenians faced the second invasion, vacating their city and their homes and taking to the "wooden walls" of the fleet; the breadth of vision which made them refuse to despair of Greece and of freedom: these were triumphs of the spirit that gave Athens, at one bound, a new position of moral hegemony over the rest of Greece. The three hundred Spartans at Thermopylae were a special breed of men. Valor had been bred and drilled into them; it was their way of life. The triumphs of Athens were of a different order. Here, for the first and perhaps the only time in Greek history, a whole people rose to the height of a great argument and lived and died like heroes.

Whence did the Athenians draw this greatness of spirit? Much, of course, has to be attributed to men like Miltiades, Aristides, and especially Themistocles. Much has to be ascribed to Solon and Pisistratus and Clisthenes, the founders. But I would suggest that the way to Athens' unique achievement was also prepared by her unique institution, tragedy. By the time of Marathon the Athenians had had over forty years of direct communion with the heroic spirit through tragedy. No other Greeks had gone to such a school, and no others behaved quite as they did. Aristophanes makes Aeschylus and Euripides agree that the tragic poet is the teacher of his people; may not the Persian Wars be the first and greatest witness to the truth of that creed?

But we cannot suppose that all Athenians were prepared to live at the height of the heroic spirit all the time. Some of them found even the tragic performances, coming once a year, too grim and unrelieved for a steady diet. The record of their protest is enshrined in the phrase *ouden pros ton Dionyson,* "nothing to do with Dionysus." [4] The explanations of this protest which we have from antiquity (the Suda and the paroemiographers) are predicated on the satyr-play theory: that is, on the notion that tragedy began as a jolly, relaxed performance by a satyr-chorus, in the Dionysiac spirit, and only acquired seriousness later. The protest, then, would have been directed against this betrayal of Dionysus. But we are not bound by the explanations. The situation is actually much simpler. Tragedy did indeed have nothing to do with Dionysus from the beginning; yet Pisistratus had made it the centerpiece of his new Dionysia. Protests may have been heard at once; certainly they were raised before long, and the very success of tragedy must have augmented them. The Dionysiac spirit of fun and self-abandonment was being overshadowed by something alien to it.

Whatever the attitude of the Pisistratids toward the complaints, it is clear that the young democracy took them seriously. Several additions were made to the Dionysiac program in less than twenty-five years, all of them calculated to restore Dionysus and his spirit to a place of honor alongside tragedy. In 509/508, immediately following the establishment of the democracy, competitions were added in the dithyramb, for men's choruses (later for boys also).[5] At a date which is not entirely certain—the most likely year is 502/501, but it may have been earlier—informal revel-choruses, *kômoi*, were included in the program, though not as a competition; and later, in 486/485, a formal competition in "comedy," *komôidia*, was instituted. But the earliest and most interesting concession to Dionysus was the introduction of satyr-drama. At this late stage of our discussion we will not spend time on the theory that satyr-play had anything to do with the origin of tragedy. On the other hand satyrs, or more properly speaking silens, *seilênoi*, appear in abundance on sixth-century Attic vases. The credit for bringing these carefree children of nature into a dramatic performance must go to Pratinas, a native of Phlius in Peloponnese. We do not know why Pratinas settled in Athens, or exactly what inspired him to organize the satyrs as the chorus of a drama, or exactly when he did it, except that it was toward the end of the sixth century.[6] But we do know, from fifth-century testimony and from a considerable body of extant plays and fragments, what kind of drama he created. Its most striking peculiarity was that the chorus was made up of satyrs but the plot, such as it was, normally centered on a hero, who appeared in full tragic costume. The tone of the piece was relaxed and humorous, but in form it was an appendage to tragedy. Satyr-plays were always written by tragic poets, never by comic poets, and differed from comedies in form, structure, and meters. Thus the crucial fact about satyr-drama is that it began and continued as a satellite of tragedy. That is the only explanation of its form and its existence. Satyr-play gave the Dionysiac spirit a place in the Dionysiac festival, but without threatening the pre-eminence of tragedy.

How are these two developments related to Aeschylus? Satyr-play was certainly in existence by the beginning of his career, and he was famous for his contributions to it.[7] It will do no harm to bear in mind, as we proceed to discuss Aeschylus' tragic genius, that it was not exclusively tragic. Like Shakespeare he could frame a jest, or plant one in the back rows, with the best of them (we must also remember that he acted the leads in his own productions, including the satyr-plays). But of course the moral function and effect of tragedy are vastly more important than satyr-play in assessing the achievement of Aeschylus. If tragedy did play a part in educating the Athenians to heroism in the Persian wars, he must have been aware of it; he may even possibly have had a hand in the process. Such a role would eminently suit the Aeschylus of Aristophanes' *Frogs*. It also suits the real Aeschylus, but in his case the question is whether it was an original motive or a later outgrowth of his experience. In any case we must be very careful how we apply the idea to him.

Indeed one must be wary of applying any fixed idea to Aeschylus. For example he called his own works "slices (portions) from Homer's great feasts," [8] and this is often cited, quite wrongly, as if it meant that he was the first tragedian to use Homeric or epic material. Aristophanes presents him as an exemplar of the good old times, and therefore he is in danger of being taken for a political and social conservative. He was a great religious poet and thinker and therefore is often compared to the Hebrew prophets and other preachers of revealed truth, or regarded as the spokesman of some cult like Orphism or that of Eleusis. Actually Aeschylus was a devotee and follower of Homer, but in a thoroughly un-Homeric way; a staunch upholder of moral and political values, but in a liberal rather than a conservative spirit; and a truly religious thinker, but not in the service of any particular cult or dogma.[9] And all these traits together do not capture the most important thing of all: that he was a tragic dramatist, the first dramatic genius in the Western world.

Much though Aeschylus has been admired as the "creator of tragedy," [10] the magnitude of his achievement as a dramatist has not been properly recognized. In part this springs from neglect, failure to study his plays carefully as plays; in part it springs from false premises, especially the *idée fixe* that tragedy was already dramatic before him and therefore all that remained for him to do was to enhance or refocus its dramatic qualities. On the contrary, and notwithstanding everything we have attributed to Thespis, it is no more than simple justice to say that Aeschylus created tragedy as we understand it: that is, as tragic drama.

It is difficult to formulate Aeschylus' achievement in brief terms, but we must essay it as a framework for the discussion that follows. Briefly, then, he began with the *pathos,* the death or suffering of the hero, which Thespis had put at the center of tragedy, and the lamentations of the chorus over it. Aeschylus accepted the *pathos* as something co-ordinate with the hero's greatness. But he was the kind of man who could not accept it, in the long run, unless it made sense: that is, unless it could be understood as flowing from certain events or conditions and issuing in others. In his search for causes Aeschylus is the Athenian counterpart, in the moral and religious sphere, of the great Milesians who "invented" philosophy in the generation or two before his birth. His spiritual kinship with Anaximander is particularly striking: not only with Anaximander's concept of a cosmic 'justice' and 'injustice,' but above all with the scope and comprehensiveness of his vision of life.[11] For an attempt to understand the world causally—whether it be the physical world or that of the spirit—necessarily leads outward in all directions. In Aeschylus' case it led to a projection outward, backward, forward, and upward from the *pathos,* in the three dimensions of space, time, and relationship to God. And this expansion brought with it in turn a series of far-reaching changes in every aspect of tragedy from stage management to theology.[12] Moreover the whole development was motivated and guided not by technical considerations but by an increasingly bold and complex intuition of the meaning of life. Aeschylus exploited the resources of the epic tradition, the poetic medium, or media, and the theater with ever-increasing mastery to serve this master purpose. He was above all a bold, imaginative experimenter, and tragic drama was the outcome, not the point of departure, of his restless experimentation.

The reader will have noticed that at this point I speak of "development," not merely of "creation." A modification of what was said previously about Aeschylus' creative act is not intended. No great creative step in literature is limited to a single act at a single moment. Very likely if we had more evidence for Thespis, and especially if we had a few of his *tragôidiai* in datable sequence, we could distinguish his "creative act" also into a series of probes or forward movements culminating in a new creation. In any case fate has willed it that we now have, in spite of the tiny selection of Aeschylus' work that is available to us, a datable sequence of plays leading to a climax. The re-dating of the *Suppliants*[13] has opened the door to a new appraisal of his activity, that is, of the restless process of experimentation spoken of just above. We have incontrovertible dates for five of the seven extant plays and a narrow range of possibilities for a sixth. Only the *Prometheus Bound* cannot be dated with any certainty or fitted into any coherent sequence.[14] The *Persians* was produced in 472; *Seven against Thebes* belongs to 467; the *Suppliants* has to be dated after 467, perhaps to 463 or in any case not much later; and the *Oresteia* is fixed at 458. Thus the *Persians* is the oldest extant play, and the entire extant dramatic work of Aeschylus—with the exception of fragments, most of them undatable,[15] and possibly the ever-bothersome *Prometheus*—is limited to a period of fourteen years near the end of his life (he died in Sicily in 456). By way of corollary, we must resign ourselves to knowing practically nothing about Aeschylus' dramaturgy during the twenty-five or more years of his career down to 472.[16] Painful though this void is, it is surely outweighed by the gain in having a relatively brief period of dramatic activity available for study, and from Aeschylus' ripest production. Later on I will suggest reasons for conjecturing that the blank years did not produce much of note or potential interest for our purpose: in other words that the vigorous experimentation I spoke of earlier, the process which led to Aeschylean drama as we know it, did in fact begin in the 470's, when the poet was fifty years old.

The rapid development which I propose to sketch in the following pages can be summarized analytically under nine headings, as follows:

(1) An increase in the *size of the acting company,* from one to two and finally to three.

(2) A more and more incisive presentation of *contrast and conflict,* not only between individuals but also on occasion between actor and chorus.

(3) An increasingly cogent *organization of episodes,* so that instead of merely disclosing or interpreting the *pathos* they lead up to it and/or away from it.

(4) An increasing intensity of focus upon the *tragic choice* which leads to the *pathos,* and upon the aura of fear and foreboding which surrounds it.

(5) Side by side with this intensification of the tragic dilemma, a more and more clearly revealed optimistic faith in its *ultimate resolution.*

(6) The appearance and increasingly effective use of the *connected trilogy* (the *Oresteia* is our sole extant example, but *Seven* and *Suppliants* also belonged to such trilogies).

(7) A far-reaching *reinterpretation of the myths.*

(8) An increasingly concentrated and effective exploitation of the *stage picture* and stage effects.

(9) A broadening of the scene of the drama in time and space, leading on occasion to the use of what I call *"virtual action."*

It should be emphasized at once that these nine points are not really separate aspects of the matter. They all hang together. What we are dealing with is in fact a complex phenomenon but at the same time a single process: a progressive deepening and broadening of Aeschylus' tragic vision which culminates in the *Oresteia.* The following discussion will therefore not follow a set order of topics; the list above is given simply for purposes of orientation and as a check against some important features of the development being overlooked in our concentration on others.

Almost the only one of the nine points for which we have independent evidence, outside the plays themselves, is that concerning the number of actors. It is all but certain that Aeschylus himself introduced the second actor, early in his career,[17] and the three earliest plays, *Persians, Seven,* and *Suppliants,* still belong to the two-actor stage. I myself believe that Aeschylus introduced the third actor also, at a later stage and for a particular reason. We will come back to the question in a moment. In any case he adopted the innovation: the *Oresteia* is written for three actors. I have also argued elsewhere[18] that the term *hypokritês,* 'actor,' literally 'answerer,' was originally coined for or applied to the second actor, not the first. But this point is not of crucial importance to our present argument. What matters is the function of the second actor, and here the evidence is very clear. The second actor is not introduced in order to conflict or contrast with the hero; he is not a hero, or even a person at all, but an instrument for extending the play in time and space. Thus in the *Persians* he is the messenger who brings the news of the long-past battle of Salamis to distant Susa, and then the Ghost of Darius who explains it; in the *Seven* he is the Scout who carries to Eteocles the news of the invading army and the seven champions, and later the Messenger who reports the death of the two brothers. Further, as the Scout he is the one who brings the approaching menace of Polynices and the Argives pointedly to bear upon Eteocles and so forces him to his crucial act. In other words the second actor, in his characteristic role as Messenger, also enables the poet to change or sharpen the hero's situation. As Professor Kitto says,[19] "The second actor makes it possible, dramatically, to set the hero in a position which not only seems, but also is, innocent. Now the situation can change; messengers bring news or heralds make proclamations, and what was safe becomes perilous." In short, the second actor not only represents a broadening and deepening of the action; he can apply the turn of the screw.

Aeschylus' use of the second actor can be understood only from the vantage point of the hero's *pathos*.[20] The purpose is not to "get an action going" on stage through conflict or even debate or discussion, but to report—and, it may be, to explain— the hero's downfall, or else lead up to it by placing him before a tragically necessary decision which will bring on the disaster. In this respect there is a notable difference between the *Persians* and the *Seven*. In the *Persians* the disaster has already taken place before the play begins; all that remains is to bring its effect and its meaning home to us. The action, so far as we can speak of an action, goes through four stages, each having a definite relation to the disaster (the battle of Salamis).[21] These stages are: (1) apprehension (the chorus and the Queen), (2) verification (the Messenger's report of the battle), (3) explanation (by the Ghost of Darius), (4) emotional realization (the frantic lamentations of Xerxes and the chorus). The play is not yet quite a drama, but Aeschylus has given it considerable dramatic life. We know that in Phrynichus' *Phoenician Women*, presented four years before, the report of the defeat came at the beginning, so that the rest of the play can have been little more than a long-drawn-out *thrênos*. Aeschylus postpones the news, then broadens and deepens its import through the magisterial words of Darius, and finally makes us see the fearful reality of the *pathos* in the utter collapse of Xerxes and of Persia. Out of the report of a past event the poet has spun, not exactly a dramatic action, but a rising curve of understanding and emotional involvement; and he has done it by dividing the *pathos,* as it were, into two: first the report of the defeat and then, at the end, the presentation of it in its full moral and emotional dimensions.

It is clear even from our limited evidence that the *Persians* went far beyond Phrynichus' play in this structuring and emotional building-up of the *pathos*—but it is also clear that the one thing the two plays had in common, aside from the laying of the scene at Susa, was the *pathos*. (Incidentally, the origin of tragedy in a *pathos* enables us to solve the well-known minor puzzle about historical subjects in Greek tragedy. We know of just three such plays in the fifth century, all before 470: the *Persians,* Phrynichus' *Phoenician Women,* and the *Capture of Miletus,* also by Phrynichus, produced in the 490's. Why do we hear of only three historical plays, and why was the experiment not repeated? Not out of aversion to historical subjects as such, but because the one thing absolutely essential to a tragedy was a *pathos* of heroic quality and scope, and fifth-century history in Greek lands provided just two such: the fall of Ionia and the defeat of Persia.)

In the *Seven against Thebes* Aeschylus makes a first stride toward the creation of a genuine tragic action. In the *Persians* the disaster had preceded the opening of the play and was only brought on stage by the messenger's report. Henceforth Aeschylus builds rising actions: sequences which lead up to the *pathos* as a climax. The novelty is not so much that the *pathos* now has its place near the end of the play—that must usually have been the case in the past—as that it is now a climactic event preceded and prepared for by other events. It is no longer merely presented or explained; it becomes part of a nexus of action.

This change is gradual rather than total and never quite reaches its full term in Aeschylus. Nevertheless it is a major change and brings with it a number of other developments. In the first place the famous Aeschylean foreboding, already well handled in the *Persians,* now has fuller and fuller scope to celebrate its triumphs. The *Agamemnon* provides the masterpiece, with *Choephoroe* and *Eumenides* falling only slightly below it. In the *Seven* the foreboding begins to extend and articulate itself and to draw into its ambit not only the chorus or a secondary person like Atossa, but the hero. The shadow of the coming *pathos* falls over all the persons of the play, as well as over us. For the chorus it remains a generalized fear and anxiety about what may happen; for the hero it takes more and more pointed form, as a moral and emotional crisis attending a *decision to act*. From having one focal point, the *pathos* itself, the drama begins to have two, the hero's act of choice and the *pathos;* the play is then a sequence of action leading through the one to the other.

Thus Aeschylus begins to introduce action into tragedy in two senses: the hero's decisive single *act,* preceded by agonized hesitation and surrounded by doubts and terrors, and the *action* as a whole, leading through the decision to the *pathos* as its climax. And this more complex pattern is further broadened and complicated by the appearance of the connected trilogy, so that the action of each play in turn forms part of a larger "whole action." The *Seven* is the surviving last play of such a trilogy and the *Suppliants* the first of another; the *Oresteia* we have complete. Thus five of the seven extant plays belong or once belonged to connected trilogies; the only one which we know did not belong to one is the *Persians*.

The action of the *Seven* centers upon two crucial happenings which are connected with each other but partly separated by the poet: the invasion of Thebes, with its attendant terror and threat of destruction to the city, and the duel and death of Eteocles and Polynices, which is the *pathos* of the play. These two themes meet in the person of Eteocles, who is both the valiant captain and defender of his city and the doomed son of Oedipus, destined to die by his brother's hand in fulfilment of his father's curse. The climax of Eteocles' plan for defending the city is the choice of a champion to face the last of the invaders, Polynices; he inevitably chooses himself and the choice leads inevitably to the *pathos*. But stated this way the action of the *Seven* sounds more unified than it is. In actuality the first two-thirds of the play is devoted almost exclusively to the war and the danger to the city, and throughout that much of it Eteocles appears almost exclusively as the resolute soldier and defender of his native land, not as the doomed tragic hero. It was this part of the *Seven* that moved Gorgias to coin the famous epithet quoted by the Aeschylus of the *Frogs* (line 1021): "A drama full of Ares." The choruses re-echo with the sights and sounds and terror of battle, and the speeches with the warlike spirit of fighting men.

Aeschylus has given this first section of the play an *éthos* and life of its own through two graphic devices of contrast (the first of many in his plays), one between the hero and the chorus, the other between the spirit of Thebes and that of the attackers. Eteocles is the complete male and natural leader, confident, purposeful, absorbed in defense measures and battle plans; the chorus is, at least for some time, a raggle-taggle group of terrified females, quaking at every sound and ready to give up the city for lost. The strong tension between these two poles is replaced after a while by another, somewhat less direct but even more significant. The Scout reports the names of the seven enemy chieftains and describes the impious blazons on their shields; Eteocles assigns to face each in turn a quiet, determined, godfearing Theban—until the climax is reached with Polynices. Here, at line 653, the other, the tragic theme breaks in upon us with a rush. Eteocles recognizes instantly that the curse of Oedipus is on the verge of fulfilment; he seizes sword and armor and after a short *kommos* with the chorus, in which his intense agitation is revealed, and an even shorter passage of stichomythy, plunges off stage to his death. The rest of the play is a report of the *pathos* and a lamentation over it.[22]

The two themes are not quite successfully joined. There is a wrench at the point where Eteocles the cool, efficient commander changes into the tormented, doomed hero, embracing his own death with morbid insistence. A similar peripety befalls the chorus: it changes without warning or apparent reason from a pack of frightened women into a wise, affectionate counsellor, almost a mother-figure, reasoning and pleading with the frenzied hero.

Another way of putting the same observation is that at the crucial moment Aeschylus wishes to present Eteocles as accepting, taking upon himself the tragic choice (to die by his brother's hand), but the handling is too abrupt and the act is not sufficiently prepared or motivated as a choice. The play falls apart in the middle. But this defect is connected with another, larger aspect of the matter. We said that the *Seven* is a remnant of a connected trilogy, and that the action of any such play also belongs to a larger whole action, that of the trilogy. The abruptness of Eteocles' decision and the relative lack of meshing between the two parts of the action are accounted for to some extent by the fact that the war situation belongs to the *Seven* alone while the *pathos* is a part, indeed the climax, of the action of the trilogy as a whole. In *Suppliants* and *Agamemnon* we can observe a similar intrusion of trilogic elements, if we may call them so, toward the end of the play, but they are more smoothly motivated.

The trilogic elements in the *Seven* are the folly of Laius (recollected by the chorus, lines 750 ff.) in begetting a son in spite of Apollo's warning; the parricide and incest of Oedipus; and Oedipus' curse on his sons, which becomes an Erinys or avenging Fury and is at last embodied in the sword, the "bitter Scythian guest" who allots the sons their patrimony: six feet of native soil to lie in. A train of crime and punishment, then, overarches the generations and brings the unfortunate race to an end. These are religious themes. But they are not in Aeschylus' trilogy because tragedy is "religious drama" or because it was played in a religious sanctuary. We said earlier that Aeschylus expanded the *pathos* in time, space, and metaphysical dimensions. He saw the heroic *pathos* as a thing of gigantic proportions, tremendous weight and depth and spread. As such it required a bigger setting than a single play, one closer in size and weight to the Homeric epic. But his motive in forging the connected trilogy was not merely a craving for bigness; it was also a desire to understand. All great things, good and bad, come from

God. Aeschylus, thorough Greek and devotee of Homer as he was, could understand actions of this compass only as a product of what has been called "dual motivation," that is, human and divine impulsion working together.[23]

But Aeschylus, unlike Homer, did not enjoy the epic bard's special privilege of descrying the working of divinity in any and every act of men. Like Solon, he could discern it only through its effects over a period of time. Solon had said:[24] "Those who escape, themselves, and the apportionment of the gods does not come upon them, one way or another it comes later: their children, guiltless, pay for their deeds, or their descendants after them."

The Aeschylean trilogy is the ultimate and only adequate realization of Solon's insight in art: a distinctively Athenian achievement, and what is more, achieved in Solon's way, by hard individual meditation on the problem. "Zeus, whoever he is, if he deign to accept that name, by it I call him. I cannot find any likeness, though I ponder all, except Zeus's, if I am truly to throw off my mind the frustrating burden." And again: "There drips from near the heart, instead of sleep, an effort that brings memories of pain; and (so) to men against their wills, in the end, comes wisdom." [25] These anguished cries of the chorus in *Agamemnon* come from Aeschylus' own heart and brain.

The *Suppliants* is the surviving first play of a lost trilogy which also included *Egyptians* and *Danaids*. Its peculiarities are so marked that one can understand and forgive the old effort to date it as early as possible. As we have seen, that dating was motivated above all by the prominent role of the chorus. The chorus is in fact the protagonist, and its utterances, sung or spoken (through its leader, the *coryphaeus*), occupy most of the play. It was natural to see here a survival of a primitive stage of "lyrical tragedy." But now that we know its date, between *Seven against Thebes* (467) and *Oresteia* (458), many things about the drama fall into place for the first time and become explicable.

To revert to the *Seven* for a moment, we saw how Aeschylus built up a potent but momentary contrast between Eteocles and the chorus—his firmness and decisiveness, their panic and wringing of hands—and another between the braggadocio of the invaders and the godfearing composure of the Theban defenders. To the first contrast the second actor contributed nothing; and he participated in the second only as a mouthpiece, the verbal channel through which an image of the attackers and their impious shield devices was conveyed to us. As a dramatist, Aeschylus clearly felt the lure of such contrasts, the potency of the dramatic tension they could engender. But the contrasts in the *Seven* are not completely organic to the main theme and its climax, the *pathos*. How could contrast, conflict, tension be built into the main action? In the *Oresteia* we see Aeschylus at the height of his powers, handling this problem as a master. The *Suppliants* represents a transitional, experimental stage.

In the *Seven* the second actor, faithful to his standard role of messenger and subaltern, could not directly serve this kind of dramatic purpose; it was achieved, so far as it was achieved directly, through confrontation of the protagonist with the chorus. Aeschylus uses the device again in the *Suppliants*. But this time, thanks to the nature of the legend (and was that perhaps the reason why he chose it?), the chorus is an integral part of the whole; it helps carry the main action not only of the play but of the trilogy. The Danaids are the timorous yet formidable virgins who are destined to gain asylum in Argos and later to marry and kill their husbands—all except one of them, Hypermestra, *splendide mendax* as Horace says, who spares her husband and ultimately, with him, founds the royal house of Argos. Thus for the trilogy as a whole the Danaids are in some sense like the house of Laius, and Hypermestra occupies the position of Eteocles, except that—significant difference —she does not die but lives and will give birth to a line of kings.

In the *Suppliants* we have an initial situation not unlike that of the *Seven:* a terrified, supplicating chorus of women confronting a king whose first thought is for his city. After narrating to us their panic flight from the sons of Aegyptus and imploring the protection of Zeus and the other gods of Argos, and after receiving instructions from their father, the Danaids carry the fight for asylum to the King, Pelasgus. Throughout this part of the play the chorus is protagonist, or co-protagonist with the King. Meanwhile their father Danaus plays a curiously subdued and colorless role. The brevity and lack of character in his speeches have often been remarked. Danaus twice gives his daughters brief lectures on deportment, he brings back the decision of the Argive assembly granting them asylum, and he espies the arrival of the Egyptian fleet; nothing more. During the long colloquy between the Danaids and the King he stands silent and ignored; the King does not even address him. Worst of all, in spite of his care for his daughters Danaus twice leaves them alone on stage, the first time so that he can go to Argos and return as messenger, the second time even more strangely (since they are left completely unprotected in the face of the Egyptian onslaught) so that he can return in his new role as the Egyptian herald.

Danaus was played by the second actor, and his strange, unroyal behavior is the best possible proof that the second actor was type-cast for subordinate roles only, especially that of Messenger. He could not play a real king or a hero. The awkwardness is noticeable in the *Suppliants*. Aeschylus makes a virtue of it in the last episode of the play by letting his Egyptian herald clash with the King, but it is a partial and forced solution. The real clash of wills, in the main episode, is between the King and the chorus. This scene is interesting and important from a number of points of view. What stands out in strongest relief is a paradox. The main dramatic issue in the play is whether the Danaids will be granted asylum in Argos. Their demand, reinforced by a threat to hang themselves to the statues of the gods, puts the King in a cleft stick. He must choose between evils: war with Egypt or pollution of his country's altars. Thus in this play the King is the specifically tragic figure. In his dilemma we recognize the elements of the Aeschylean tragic choice: mental anguish, hesitation between two lines of conduct both of which involve wrong and suffering. Pelasgus prefigures Agamemnon faced by the slaying of his daughter and Orestes hesitating to kill his mother. But there is something faintly unsatisfactory about Pelasgus' tragic dilemma, and the reason is that he is not the hero of the trilogy as a whole (we do not even know whether he appeared again, in the second play). For the trilogy as a whole the carrier of the tragic idea is the chorus. Their hatred of marriage and men led in the second or third play to the murder of their husbands, the sons of Aegyptus; and at that point the tragic mantle must have descended upon Hypermestra. She was the one bride who shouldered the full moral weight of the tragic choice—and chose to spare her husband.

What all this signifies is that Aeschylus' growing desire to shape each play as an action, in terms of conflict leading to a tragic choice and thence to a *pathos,* is partially crossed by his equally strong desire to subsume these actions under a whole, the trilogy, as parts of a larger action guided and ultimately resolved by the gods. The difficulty has different aspects for the parts and for the whole. On the one hand Aeschylus has only one actor (himself!) available for major roles. Hence he tries to achieve his dramatic conflict by pitting the protagonist against the chorus. But if the protagonist happens to be a secondary person for the theme of the trilogy, as Pelasgus is, a certain obliquity and loss of momentum is bound to result. On the other hand choruses are inherently unfitted to play a protagonist's role, and few Greek myths provided groups of either men or women which could be used for this purpose at all.

Aeschylus exploited the possibilities in *Suppliants* and again in *Eumenides,* but such a method could not be adopted as the normal one. And actually, from what we know of the Danaid trilogy it is apparent, or at least arguable, that he had to abandon it before the end. Hypermestra must have emerged at last from the anonymity of the chorus as *the* tragic heroine. For the tragic choice is necessarily made by an individual.

Thus the choral gambit was not really satisfactory, except for special cases like the *Eumenides.* A tragic conflict can be properly realized only by two individuals of approximately equal stature, and since the second actor was irrevocably cast as Messenger, Herald, and the like, the only way out was—a third actor. Aeschylus may have pondered this solution while he was working on the Danaid trilogy; in any case he had adopted it by the time of the *Oresteia.* And I reiterate my earlier suggestion[26] that he, rather than Sophocles, was responsible for the innovation; for it was his development as a dramatist that made the third actor necessary.

But we are not through with the difficulties created by the connected trilogy. Pelasgus was faced with a tragic choice; the chorus and Hypermestra were faced with another; and the murder of the Egyptian husbands was certainly a *pathos,* though not an individual one. But the trilogy as a whole did not end with a *pathos;* it ended with good auguries for Lynceus, Hypermestra, and Argos, and a ringing speech by Aphrodite, part of which is still preserved, affirming the holiness and divinely sanctioned status of marriage. The parallel with the *Oresteia* is striking: that is, the parallel with Athena's great speeches in the last play, to the court of the Areopagus and the Eumenides, affirming the sanctity of law and predicting the future prosperity of Athens. This happy outcome of a tragic action is a great paradox, and a peculiarly Aeschylean paradox. We are not talking here about happy endings in Euripides' manner, tacked on to the ends of plays. The outcomes of the

Danaid trilogy and the *Oresteia* signify something that goes beyond the particular story and the particular occasion: not shallow optimism or desire for a momentary dramatic satisfaction, but a deep faith that the gods, Zeus above all, will ultimately help men find their way to reason and happiness. Aeschylus' optimism is a very personal, hardly won faith, and it is focused upon individuals but also upon institutions. Religion, marriage, the rule of law, are the pillars of civilized community life. They have to be won and sustained by hard effort in the face of tragic dilemmas and sufferings; for men only learn through suffering. "It was Zeus who set mortals' feet on the path, he who established the binding law, 'Through suffering, learning,' " sings the chorus in *Agamemnon* 176–178.

Pathei mathos. The famous phrase has a grandeur worthy of tragedy, and yet it is untragic, even anti-tragic. Not that Aeschylus depreciated the tragic suffering. No man ever knew the dark depths of fear and anguish, or the compulsion to lament over greatness lost, more profoundly than he. Mme. de Romilly[27] has shown in detail how graphically Aeschylus presents the symptoms of fear and perturbation. But she also shows that the tragic anguish is the sign of gods at work. It is their way of opening a man's heart to learning. At the beginning of *Agamemnon* the old men of the chorus fear they know not what, with a fear that is abysmal, confused, endless and undefined; at the end of *Eumenides* we have learned through the teaching of Athena to feel a beneficent and pious fear, a deep respect for law and for the gods. The hymn to Zeus, from which I quoted a moment ago, comes in the middle of the opening chorus of the *Agamemnon*. There the dark clouds of fear are penetrated by a ray of faith, but only for a moment; then they close in again. In the *Eumenides* they reappear in far more real and terrible guise in the persons of the Furies themselves; but at the end of the play and the trilogy these have been transformed, through the will of Zeus and the persuasions of Athena (*i.e.,* of reason), into the august but smiling Kindly Ones, the *Eu*menides. The ray of light has finally transformed darkness itself into light, a sun of tranquillity and blessing for men.

Similarly in the *Suppliants* the chorus is agitated at the beginning by a cloud of nameless, irrational fears. It is upheld only by its faith in Zeus, which however is deplorably unenlightened and misguided. These young women are naïve enough to think that Zeus will sustain them in hating all men forever! Here too the terror and confusion of the beginning are the necessary preparation for Zeus's final message of reconciliation and happiness, delivered this time by Aphrodite.

The parallel between the two trilogies (which incidentally helps to strengthen the new dating of the Danaid trilogy) shows us a strange paradox in the development of Aeschylus' dramaturgy. The dramatic instinct which led him more and more to center the actions of his plays upon strife and conflict, led him at the same time beyond them. The drama of conflict between mortals is overshadowed and subsumed in the trilogy as a whole by the vaster drama of the resolution of mortal conflict by the gods. One necessary result is that the *pathos* of the individual hero bulks less large in the whole. Not only does the trilogy no longer end with a *pathos*—the Theban trilogy ended with the death of Eteocles, the *Oresteia* ends with Athena and the Eumenides: Orestes is gone and forgotten—but the intermediate *pathê* also lose some of their sting and finality. Agamemnon's death will bring his avenger, Clytemestra's death brings hers—and, in due time, the final redemption.

These displacements are reflected concretely in what happens to the *thrênoi,* the lamentations over the dead hero. *Persians* and *Seven* end with ritualistic *thrênoi* of a very old kind, showing the traditional elements of form which were studied by Peretti. Earlier in both plays the epirrhematic form which characterized the *thrênoi* is put to more flexible and more specifically dramatic use, in the *kommoi* or lyric exchanges between Messenger and chorus (*Persians*), Eteocles and chorus (*Seven*).

This process continues in the *Suppliants*. In the *Oresteia* the epirrhematic form is used again and again with superb dramatic effect: in the Cassandra scene, in the confrontation of Clytemestra and the chorus after the murder, in the songs of the Eumenides. The old undramatic *pathos* and the static forms of lamentation that accompanied it have been caught up in the service of a larger unity, an ongoing movement. *Pathos* has become a part of the drama and ultimately gives way to *mathos,* learning.

I should like to single out just one feature of the *Agamemnon* for special comment: its plot. The action of the play, though simple in Aristotle's sense, that is, lacking a peripety or sudden reversal, is complex and subtle to a degree. Most striking of all is the fact that most of the events which constitute the action do not actually take place *in* it. The crucial tragic choice which dominates the play was made ten years before, at Aulis, and is reported in the first great chorus: Agamemnon's decision to slay his daughter Iphigenia. This first killing is followed and overtopped by the mass slaughter at Troy, seen intuitively by Clytemestra and reflected upon by the chorus; by the original crime of Paris and Helen and its acceptance by the Trojans, again reflected upon by the chorus; and by the fearful loss of life among the returning Argives in the storm on the Aegaean, reported by the Herald. Thus when Agamemnon finally sets foot on stage he is accompanied by a long train of ghosts: men and women perished, blood spilled, a great city ruined, in a dubious cause. All that actually happens on the stage is that he returns, treads a purple carpet, enters his palace, and is murdered. But the carpet symbolizes, by a stroke of dramatic genius, all the blood he has shed or helped to shed. His crimes and those of others, added together, constitute the "virtual action"; all are part of it and all are present when he treads the carpet. Before he dies Cassandra penetrates still further into the past: she sees the slaughtered children of Thyestes holding their own flesh in their hands, and smells the charnel-house stench of the palace. Thus in *Agamemnon* the dramatic action has expanded in time and space and taken into itself, in "virtual" form, a whole generation and more of crimes and sufferings, at Argos, Sparta, Aulis, Troy, and on the Aegean: the miseries of two whole nations spread over many years. This is the dreadful burden of evil—made heavier still by two more crimes, those of Clytemestra and Orestes—which the gods must help men to overcome and transform into good at last. For the spiritual energy to carry out such a superhuman work of transformation can come only from God.

The *Oresteia* is Aeschylus' acknowledged masterpiece in every dramatic element: tense and sustained foreboding, superb choruses, a new and subtler use of messenger's speeches, the figure of Clytemestra, the magnificently dramatic idea of the purple carpet, Cassandra's piercing visions, the confrontation of Clytemestra and the chorus, the great evocation of Agamemnon's spirit in the *Choephoroe,* the Furies, and all the rest. Here conflict reaches a new level of tension, the *pathê* come as shattering climaxes. Yet the discrepancy remains between the *pathos*-centered individual play and the redemption-centered whole. It is no accident that most modern readers find *Agamemnon* more satisfying, more tragic, than *Choephoroe* and *Eumenides*. It is also a fact that the action is better organized and focused, as an *actual* sequence of events, in the second and third plays. In any case the *Oresteia* is the culmination of Aeschylus' dramaturgy, and the anomalies we have noticed are embodied in a whole of such enormous sweep and power that we lesser mortals ought to criticize them, if criticize them we must, on our knees.

At the end, instead of commenting further on the *Oresteia* I should like to return to two larger questions that directly concern us: why Aeschylus created the tragic action and the trilogy. I believe that these two poles of his achievement, in spite of the tension between them, are interrelated and spring from a common source, the experience of Athens in the Persian

Wars. It may be a coincidence that all the extant plays date from after the Wars, but I do not think so. Further, although we cannot date any connected trilogy except the three we have discussed, I should like to propose the hypothesis that the others (we know of six or seven more)[28] likewise date from the last fifteen or twenty years of Aeschylus' life.

We have already remarked on the Solonian spirit of the Aeschylean connected trilogy, with its demonstration of God's justice at the end: "For no man escapes *his* watchful eye, and surely in the end his justice is made manifest." But true as this is, the affinity with Solon is not a matter of direct inheritance through the development of tragedy itself. There is no evidence and no reason to believe that the Solonian theodicy had any place in tragedy before Aeschylus. And we have already seen that the tragic action, in any proper sense, only begins to develop after the *Persians*.

In explaining Thespis' invention of *tragôidia* we had to look for a new spiritual impulse which could bring the heroic tradition back to life, and we found it, or at least a matrix for it, in the new unity of Athens forged by Solon and cemented by Pisistratus, linking noble to commoner. The result, in tragedy, was the bringing of an heroic *pathos* from the distant past directly into the present. To add to this *pathos* the new dimensions of *action* and *trilogy* required a spiritual energy at least equal to that which had animated Thespis, and a source of that energy in a new way of seeing and feeling heroic action and suffering. Such insights are given to a people only when it itself has undergone an ordeal of heroic proportions, and that was granted to Athens just once, in the Persian Wars. I have suggested that the spirit of Athens in those years had already been shaped in part by tragedy. But the Wars in turn were the root from which her new greatness flowered, and one of its earliest fruits was Aeschylean tragedy, with its strange mixture of tragic insight and deep confidence in the ultimate goodness of the world. In the years of Marathon and Salamis the consciousness of living at the height of great events became, for the first time in recorded history, the common property of a whole people. Phrynichus had touched the spring of tragic feeling, too painfully, with his *Capture of Miletus*. More trying —and bracing—years followed. What an intelligent and sensitive observer could now perceive was the connection between men's choices and their fates; for as they chose so they fared. And what a religious observer could perceive was that the whole complex web of choices and actions and sufferings had been under the watchful eye of the gods from the beginning; for in the end it was they who brought victory and justice out of disaster. The Wars even had a trilogic structure. The first act of the drama, unrelievedly tragic, ended with the fall of Miletus; the second led to the miracle of Marathon; the third, awaited with long foreboding and played out before the eyes of Greece and the world, culminated at Salamis. How could a born dramatist like Aeschylus, living in such a time, fail to catch the dramatic rhythm of these happenings, or the interconnection in them between human choices and sufferings on the one hand and divine justice on the other? The Persian Wars, the long ordeal of Greece, and her salvation through the spirit of Athens and the will of the gods, are the prototype of the *Oresteia*.

Aeschylus died in Sicily. We have his epitaph, written— perhaps—by himself. It does not speak of his plays or his dramatic career, only of his service in the Wars. But the spirit and the secret of his drama lives in it: "Aeschylus, Euphorion's son, Athenian, lies in this tomb, perished in wheat-bearing Gela. Of his valor and fair fame the sacred grove of Marathon can tell, and the long-haired Persian who learned to know it there."

APPENDIX

NOTES

INDEX

Appendix: Selected Greek Texts

1. Ar. *Poet.* 4, 1449a9–11: γενομένη δ' οὖν ἀπ' ἀρχῆς αὐτοσχεδιαστικῆς, καὶ αὐτὴ καὶ ἡ κωμῳδία, καὶ ἡ μὲν ἀπὸ τῶν ἐξαρχόντων τὸν διθύραμβον, . . .

2. *Ibid.* 18–21: (ἔτι δὲ τὸ μέγεθος) ἐκ μικρῶν μύθων καὶ λέξεως γελοίας διὰ τὸ ἐκ σατυρικοῦ μεταβαλεῖν ὀψὲ ἀπεσεμνύνθη.

3. Themist. *Orat.* 26, p. 816d: οὐ προσέχομεν Ἀριστοτέλει ὅτι τὸ μὲν πρῶτον ὁ χορὸς εἰσιὼν ᾖδεν εἰς τοὺς θεούς, Θέσπις δὲ πρόλογόν τε καὶ ῥῆσιν ἐξεῦρεν, . . . ;

4. Archil. fr. 77 Diehl: ὡς Διωνύσοι' ἄνακτος καλὸν ἐξάρξαι μέλος | οἶδα διθύραμβον, οἴνῳ ξυγκεραυνωθεὶς φρένας.

5. Hdt. 1, 23: λέγουσι Κορίνθιοι . . . Ἀρίονα . . . διθύραμβον πρῶτον ἀνθρώπων τῶν ἡμεῖς ἴδμεν ποιήσαντά τε καὶ ὀνομάσαντα καὶ διδάξαντα ἐν Κορίνθῳ.

6. Suda s. v. Ἀρίων: . . . λέγεται καὶ τραγικοῦ τρόπου εὑρετὴς γενέσθαι, καὶ πρῶτος χορὸν στῆσαι καὶ διθύραμβον ἆσαι καὶ ὀνομάσαι τὸ ἀδόμενον ὑπὸ τοῦ χοροῦ, καὶ σατύρους εἰσενεγκεῖν ἔμμετρα λέγοντας.

7. Ioannes Diaconus, *Comm. in Hermogenem, Rhein. Mus.* 63 (1908) 150: τῆς δὲ τραγῳδίας πρῶτον δρᾶμα Ἀρίων ὁ Μηθυμναῖος εἰσήγαγεν, ὥσπερ Σόλων ἐν ταῖς ἐπιγραφομέναις Ἐλεγείαις ἐδίδαξε. Δράκων δὲ ὁ Λαμψακηνὸς δρᾶμά φησι πρῶτον Ἀθήνησι διδαχθῆναι ποιήσαντος Θέσπιδος.

8. Hdt. 5, 67, 5: τά τε δὴ ἄλλα οἱ Σικυώνιοι ἐτίμων τὸν Ἄδρηστον καὶ δὴ πρὸς τὰ πάθεα αὐτοῦ τραγικοῖσι χοροῖσι ἐγέραιρον, τὸν μὲν Διόνυσον οὐ τιμῶντες, τὸν δὲ Ἄδρηστον. Κλεισθένης δὲ χοροὺς μὲν τῷ Διονύσῳ ἀπέδωκε, τὴν δὲ ἄλλην θυσίην Μελανίππῳ.

9. Zenobius (*Corpus Paroemiogr. Graec.*) V 40: Οὐδὲν πρὸς τὸν Διόνυσον. ἐπειδὴ τῶν χορῶν ἐξ ἀρχῆς εἰθισμένων διθύραμβον ᾄδειν εἰς τὸν Διόνυσον, οἱ ποιηταὶ ὕστερον ἐκβάντες τὴν συνήθειαν ταύτην Αἴαντας καὶ Κενταύρους γράφειν ἐπεχείρησαν. ὅθεν οἱ θεώμενοι σκώπτοντες ἔλεγον, Οὐδὲν πρὸς τὸν Διόνυσον. διὰ γοῦν τοῦτο τοὺς σατύρους ὕστερον ἔδοξεν αὐτοῖς προεισάγειν, ἵνα μὴ δοκῶσιν ἐπιλανθάνεσθαι τοῦ θεοῦ.

10. Suda s. v. Οὐδὲν πρὸς τὸν Διόνυσον: Ἐπιγένους . . . βέλτιον δὲ οὕτως. τὸ πρόσθεν εἰς τὸν Διόνυσον γράφοντες τούτοις ἠγωνίζοντο, ἅπερ καὶ σατυρικὰ ἐλέγετο. ὕστερον δὲ μεταβάντες εἰς τὸ τραγῳδίας γράφειν, κατὰ μικρὸν εἰς μύθους καὶ ἱστορίας ἐτράπησαν, μηκέτι τοῦ Διονύσου μνημονεύοντες. ὅθεν τοῦτο καὶ ἐπεφώνησαν. καὶ Χαμαιλέων ἐν τῷ Περὶ Θέσπιδος τὰ παραπλήσια ἱστορεῖ.

Notes

BIBLIOGRAPHICAL NOTE

The most important recent surveys of the problem treated here are listed in chapter I, note 4.

A very few works are cited in the book in abbreviated form:

Pick.-Camb., *DTC* = Arthur W. Pickard-Cambridge, *Dithyramb Tragedy and Comedy* (Oxford 1927); *DTC²* = second edition revised by T. B. L. Webster (Oxford 1962).

Id., *Dr. Fest.* = Sir Arthur Pickard-Cambridge, *The Dramatic Festivals of Athens* (Oxford 1953).

Schmid, *Gr. Lit.* = Wilhelm Schmid, *Geschichte der griechischen Literatur*, Handbuch der Altertumswissenschaft, VII 1 (Munich, vol. I, 1929; vol. II, 1934).

Lesky, *Trag. Dicht.* = Albin Lesky, *Die tragische Dichtung der Hellenen* (Göttingen 1956), especially chaps. I, "Die Ursprungsprobleme," pp. 11–38, and II, "Thespis," pp. 39–44.

Else, *A.'s Poet.* = Gerald F. Else, *Aristotle's Poetics: The Argument* (Cambridge, Mass. 1957).

Id., "Origin" = id., "The Origin of ΤΡΑΓΩΙΔΙΑ", *Hermes* 85 (1957) 19–46.

The fundamental importance of the works of Pickard-Cambridge and Lesky is indicated repeatedly in the text and notes. Schmid's volumes—consulted, I fear, more often than read—are basic in a different way. Not so much what he has specifically to say about the origin of tragedy as the view he gives of the spirit of "Altattika" and its literature, especially in volume I, pp. 363–371 (Solon), and volume II, pp. 5–32 ("Vorbereitung der attischen Literatur"), provides a frame and a guide for my theory. (Similarly, although it is not listed above, anyone who hopes to arrive at a truly viable theory of the origin of tragedy should read and reread and ponder the first few pages of the chapter on Aeschylus in the first volume of Werner Jaeger's *Paideia*.)

My book and article are cited here solely for convenience. The article gives important background to the views set forth in these pages, and fuller discussion of some details.

INTRODUCTION

1. See n. 8 below.

2. *The Idea of a Theatre* (Princeton 1949) 26. Fergusson refers in his footnote to Jane Harrison's *Ancient Art and Ritual* (Cambridge 1913) and her *Themis* (Cambridge 1912; now available in paperback) with its "Excursus on the ritual forms preserved in Greek Tragedy" by Murray (pp. 341–363). But the theory has always been identified particularly with the name of Gilbert Murray (an Oxonian all his life, by the way). On it see below, pp. 27–28. Another recent book on tragedy which accepts the theory, but with judicious caveats and retrenchments, is Herbert J. Muller's *The Spirit of Tragedy* (New York 1956); see pp. 25–26, 30–31, 89–92 (with references to Fergusson). Murray himself came closer to the mark when he talked in other terms: *The Classical Tradition in Poetry* (Cambridge, Mass. 1927) 239: "In plays like *Hamlet* or the *Agamemnon* or the *Electra* . . . we have also, I suspect, a strange unanalyzed vibration below the surface, an undercurrent of desires and fears and passions, long slumbering yet eternally familiar, which have for thousands of years lain near the root of our most intimate emotions . . ." Cf. Muller, *Spirit of Tragedy*, 35. This, and not a ritual form, is what the Greek tragedians (no doubt unconsciously) presupposed and worked with.

3. Arthur W. (later Sir Arthur) Pickard-Cambridge, *Dithyramb Tragedy and Comedy* (Oxford 1927). This is the classic treatment of the subject not only in English but in any language, in the sense of a truly critical review of the evidence and judgment of what it is worth and what it indicates. My indebtedness to it is profound. The second edition, edited by Professor T. B. L. Webster of London (Oxford 1962), adds much valuable material but does not replace the original.

4. Webster, *DTC*[2] 128–129, retains it in modified form. T. H. Gaster's *Thespis: Ritual, Myth and Drama in the Ancient Near East* (New York 1950) proves nothing for Greece, and especially for Athens.

5. For a searching critique of the idea of ritual expectancy in Sophocles see G. M. Kirkwood, *A Study of Sophoclean Drama* (Cornell Studies in Classical Philology, vol. XXXI, Ithaca 1958) 12–16.

6. E.g., Emil Reisch in *Festschrift Theodor Gomperz dargebracht* (Vienna 1902) 469–471; Walther Kranz, *Stasimon* (Berlin 1933) 12–19.

7. See below, pp. 87–88.

8. We owe the new dating to a tiny scrap of papyrus containing parts of five lines of a *didaskalia* or record of the competitions (*Oxyrhynchus Papyri*, vol. XX, no. 2256 frag. 3; most conveniently available in Gilbert Murray's

INTRODUCTION 109

Oxford Classical Text edition of Aeschylus, 2nd ed. [Oxford 1955] 2). Scant though it is, it refers unmistakably to *Danaids* and *Amymone* (a satyr-play), which we already knew to be the last two plays of the tetralogy that began with the *Suppliants;* and it designates Aeschylus as winner over Sophocles with this tetralogy. Since Sophocles first competed in 468, with a victory, and Aeschylus won in 467 with the tetralogy which included the *Seven,* the earliest available year for the new victory is 466. The fragmentary first line of the *didaskalia* may point to 463; in any case we can hardly go lower than 460 (*Oresteia* 458). Murray, Pohlenz, and others have vigorously contested the new dating, suggesting that the papyrus is unreliable; that the trilogy might have been written much earlier though not actually performed until the 460's; that the reference might be to a victory won with Aeschylus's plays after his death, by his son or grandson; and so on. Against these attempts to wriggle out of the consequences, it seems to me that Lesky, *Hermes* 82 (1954) 1–13 and *Trag. Dicht.* 59–60, has definitely established the authenticity and authority of the fragment. But even if it should end by being discredited I would hold to the ideological and structural arguments repeatedly urged by Walter Nestle (see next note).

9. References in Lesky, *Trag. Dicht.* 60 n. 1; see also the remarks of Nestle's pupil Walter Jens, *Die Stichomythie in der frühen griechischen Tragödie,* Zetemata, XI 11 n. 1 (Munich 1955).

10. A special chapter under that title was devoted to the *Suppliants* in the first two editions of Professor Kitto's widely known book (H. D. F. Kitto, *Greek Tragedy* [London, ed. 1 1939, ed. 2 1950]. In the third edition (1961) the chapter is partly rewritten but the title—and the isolation of the play from the rest of Aeschylus' work—remains. In the first two editions the first sentence of the chapter, and the book, ran: "The great interest that the *Supplices* has for us lies not in its primitiveness but in its maturity." This statement (exact in every detail, in my opinion) is not belied by Professor Kitto's treatment in the third edition.

11. For the ideas which animated this production see the fascinating account by its directors, Tyrone Guthrie and Tanya Moiseiwitsch, in *Thrice the Brinded Cat Hath Mew'd* (Toronto 1955) 111–178, especially 116–118, 153–155, including the following remark (p. 117): "Just as the participants at Holy Communion commemorate Christ's sacrifice, so, presumably, the Athenian audience at the Dionysiac festival partook of the Passion there commemorated."

12. To such an extent that Karl Jaspers was impelled to say *Tragedy is Not Enough* (Boston 1952) (actually an excerpt from Jaspers' larger work, hitherto untranslated, entitled *Von der Wahrheit*).

13. Jerome S. Bruner, *The Process of Education* (Cambridge, Mass. 1960) 46, 53.

14. See for example Herbert Weisinger, *Tragedy and the Fortunate Fall* (East Lansing, Mich., 1953); H. J. Muller (see above, n. 2); D. D. Raphael, *The Paradox of Tragedy* (London 1960); Oscar Mandel, *A Definition of Tragedy* (New York 1961); Elder Olson, *Tragedy and the Theory of Drama*

(Detroit 1961); George Steiner, *The Death of Tragedy* (New York 1961). On the whole question see also the eloquent and important remarks of Harald Patzer, *Die Anfänge der griechischen Tragödie* (Wiesbaden 1962) 1–10.

Chapter I. Dionysus, Goat-Men, and *Tragóidia*

1. Translated by Clifton Fadiman in *The Philosophy of Nietzsche* (Modern Library, New York n.d.) 985.

2. Itself intended, according to Wagner's own explicit testimony, as a rebirth of Greek, especially Aeschylean, tragedy. He wrote in 1847, after prolonged study of Aeschylus (R. Wagner, *Mein Leben*, Volksausgabe ed. 2 [Munich 1915] II 169): "Nothing could equal the sublime emotion which the *Agamemnon* called forth in me; until the end of the *Eumenides* I remained in a state of transport from which I have never really returned or become reconciled to modern literature. My ideas on the significance of the drama, and of the theatre in particular, were decisively shaped by these experiences." (Further refs. in Schmid, *Gr. Lit.* II 307 n.7.)

3. Perhaps it needs to be said again, with emphasis, that what is proposed in this book is a theory. With the evidence we have available, no one can honestly claim to offer anything more. Demonstration is out of the question.

4. I have already said (Introd., n. 3) that Pickard-Cambridge's *Dithyramb Tragedy and Comedy* is the classic survey of the evidence. The canonical treatment of the current state of the problem is the chapter on "Die Ursprungsprobleme" (note the plural) in Albin Lesky's *Tragische Dichtung;* see Bibliographical Note, p. 107. T. B. L. Webster briefly reviews the recent history of the question in *Fifty Years of Classical Scholarship* (Oxford 1954) 80–83. A fuller account, uneven but often interesting and beginning much farther back, is given by C. del Grande in ΤΡΑΓΩΙΔΙΑ (Naples 1952) 255–289. Finally, and in greatest detail for the recent theories, Harald Patzer, *Die Anfänge der griechischen Tragödie* (Wiesbaden 1962) 39–88.

5. App. 1 (*i.e.*, Appendix [p. 105], item no. 1).

6. Wilamowitz, *Einleitung in die griechische Tragödie*, ed. 2 (Berlin 1910) 64, rendered *tón exarchontón ton dithyrambon* by "den sängern des dithyrambos," *i.e.*, the chorus; necessarily so, since Wilamowitz believed that the individual standing over against the chorus was only introduced by Thespis. But there cannot really be much doubt that *exarchontón* here means individual "leaders-off," like Archilochus. For the meaning of the word see my *A.'s Poet.* 157–159. The plural is no obstacle; Aristotle is thinking of a number of such *exarchontes,* including, probably, Arion (cf. *ibid.* 160). See also Lesky, *Trag. Dicht.* 17.

7. App. 4.

8. Schmid, *Gr. Lit.* II 38 n. 5.

9. See below, p. 22.

10. App. 3.

11. Led by Schmid, *Gr. Lit.* II 38 n. 4, 775–777; M. P. Nilsson, *Neue Jahr-*

bücher f. das klass. Alt. 27 (1911) 609–613, = *Opuscula Selecta* I (Lund 1951) 61–68; Raffaele Cantarella, *Eschilo* (Florence 1941) 41–42.

12. *A's Poet.,* chap. IV, especially pp. 146–153.

13. Harold Cherniss, *Aristotle's Criticism of Presocratic Philosophy* (Baltimore 1935) chap. VII, "Aristotle and the History of Presocratic Philosophy," especially pp. 347–357. John J. Keaney has now traced the same pattern in the Aristotelian *Constitution of the Athenians: Harv. Stud. in Class. Philol.* 67 (1963) 115–146, especially 117–120, 136–139.

14. Pickard-Cambridge concludes, *DTC* 128, "he [Aristotle] was probably using that liberty of theorizing which those modern scholars who ask us to accept him as infallible have certainly not abandoned."—A reasoned view of the origin of a specific literary genre such as tragedy, or even the raising of the question, is inconceivable before the fourth century and the Lyceum. The fifth century may have entertained the question "Who was the inventor (*heuretês,* 'finder') of tragedy?" (cf. Plato, *Rep.* 10. 595 c, 598 d, 607 a; *Theaet.* 152 e: Homer the father of tragedy), but not as a historical problem.

15. It was Wilamowitz who insisted on the distinction between Aristotle's facts and his theories, *Einleitung* (see above, n. 6) 49: "was er uns als geschichtliche tatsache übermittelt, das sind wir verpflichtet als solche gelten zu lassen, so lange sich nicht der irrtum beweisen lässt: die beurteilung der tatsachen und die daraus abgezogenen allgemeinen gesetze haben nicht die geringste verbindlichkeit."

16. *DTC* 19–22, 131–135; and see my *A.'s Poet.* 159–160.

17. App. 5.

18. See next paragraph. Another variation of the same idea is that tragedy, comedy, and satyr-drama all grew from the same primitive performance, called *trygôidia* (from *tryx, trygos,* 'wine-lees' or 'new wine'): e.g., Athenaeus 2, 40 a-b: "From drunkenness came the invention of both comedy and tragedy, at Icarios [or Icarion] in Attica, and at the very time of the vintage." Similar accounts or allusions appear in Plutarch's *On the Proverbs of the Alexandrians,* chap. XXX, in the *Etymologicum Magnum,* and in John the Deacon on Hermogenes; see *DTC* 101–107.

19. Hesiod fr. 198 Rzach.

20. App. 2.

21. Max Pohlenz, *Nachrichten Gött. Akad. Phil.-Hist. Kl.* (1926) 298 n. 1, wanted to distinguish between this early " 'satyr-haftes,' mehr heiteres Spiel" and the actual satyr-drama of the fifth century; but the idea is very vague. Lesky, *Trag. Dicht.* 15 n.6, follows Gudeman in putting the definite article before Aristotle's *satyrikou* ("from the *satyrikon*"), but the basis (an inference from the Arabic translation of the *Poetics*) is highly uncertain.

22. *A.'s Poet.* 166–179.

23. *DTC*[2] 96 n. 4.

24. App. 6.

25. App. 5.

26. Lesky, *Trag. Dicht.* 31: ". . . eine Unschärfe des Ausdruckes, auf den weitere Schlüsse zu bauen nicht erlaubt ist." I would add that the use of "speaking," *legein*, where one expects "singing," *áidein*, is precisely the same Byzantine confusion as that in the spurious parts of chap. XII of the *Poetics*: see *A.'s Poet.* 362–363. To the Byzantines, speaking and singing (i.e., in classical lyric poetry and tragic choruses) were all one: they saw the same bare text in both cases and read it alike.

27. App. 7.

28. Cf. n. 14 above and pp. 23–24 below.

29. See M. P. Nilsson, *Neue Jahrbücher* 27 (1911) 611 n. 1. —H. Patzer's book *Die Anfänge der griechischen Tragödie* (Wiesbaden 1962) is a sober, careful study and avoids many of the pitfalls of the conventional theory. Thus Patzer is clear that tragedy cannot be derived from any kind of satyr performance; he emphasizes that there is no direct bridge leading from goats, *tragoi*, to *tragóidia;* and he rightly rejects any hypothesis which postulates a change from gay to solemn (*apesemnynthê*, in the usual interpretation). Yet he is led by the presumed remark of Solon to suppose that Arion invented a third kind of performance (*'Urtragödie,'* corresponding to the "tragic mode" in the Suda [App. 6]), in addition to the literary dithyramb and the satyr-performances, and that this was subsequently transmitted to Attica alongside both the others. Such a multiplication of forms only complicates the problem and, as Patzer's own attempt at an etymological explanation (pp. 131–133) shows, leaves it less clear than ever why the genre was called *tragóidia*.

30. App. 8.

31. *Apedóke*, "gave back" or "rendered," not implying that the choruses had previously been sung to Dionysus and were now being restored to him, but that Herodotus—from the point of view of fifth-century Athenian practice—regarded "tragic choruses" as naturally belonging to Dionysus.

32. *DTC* 137.

33. Webster in *DTC*², pp. 103–104, brings arguments—not convincing, it seems to me—for the *possibility* of their having been performed by "fat men" and/or satyrs.

34. App. 9 and 10; cf. *DTC* 167.

35. Cf. Zenobius, App. 9: "The choruses being accustomed from (or, in) the beginning to sing a (the) dithyramb to Dionysus, the poets later abandoned this practice and undertook to write *Ajaxes* and *Centaurs*. Hence the spectators began saying in jest, 'Nothing to do with Dionysus.' "

36. "And Chamaeleon says the same kind of thing in his book *On Thespis"* would seem at first sight to imply that Chamaeleon was not the source of what immediately precedes; but the inference is more than uncertain. It is at least as likely that Chamaeleon was the ultimate source but Photius, the immediate source of the Suda's information, drew it from an earlier compilation where Chamaeleon's name was associated with it in some indirect or ambiguous way. See Lesky, *Trag. Dicht.* 19 n. 4.

37. *Trag. Dicht.* 23.

38. See below, n. 59.

39. F. Brommer, *Satyroi* (Würzburg 1937); *id., Satyrspiele*, ed. 2 (Berlin

1959); E. Buschor, "Satyrtänze und frühes Drama," *Sitzungsberichte Bayer. Akad.* (Munich 1943) Heft 5; Webster in *DTC²*, 112–124, with other references.

40. *DTC²* 114–115.

41. See above, n. 19.

42. Shown in Brommer, *Satyroi* 61; cf. *DTC²*, "List of Monuments," no. 72; T. B. L. Webster, "Monuments Illustrating Tragedy and Satyr-Play," *U. of London Inst. of Classical Studies Bulletin,* Suppl. no. 14 (1962).

43. The distinction between "satyrs" and "silens" is secondary; see Webster, *DTC²* 117; M. P. Nilsson, *Gesch. d. gr. Religion* I, ed. 2, 232–235.

44. I.e., as satyr-drama.

45. The nearest approach to a connection is in the passage of Athenaeus already quoted above, n. 18, deriving both tragedy and comedy from the vintage festival at Icarios, the spot where Dionysus first landed in Attica. But Athenaeus does not actually mention either Thespis or the dithyramb or satyrs.

46. A number of writers, del Grande, Lesky, and others, have made a distinction between the "prehistory" and the "history" of tragedy, but one does not see that this disjunction is really fruitful until it leads inquirers to ask whether the prehistory is so constituted as to provide a firm base for the history. Otherwise it is a purely fanciful exercise.

47. *A.'s Poet.* 107–108, 119–120.

48. For Arion see above, n. 16; for Epigenes, R. C. Flickinger, *The Greek Theater and its Drama* (Chicago 1918) 12–15 (Flickinger does as much for Epigenes as can well be done). Aristotle himself said, according to Themistius (*Orat.* 27, p. 406 Dindorf), that "Sicyonian poets were the inventors of tragedy, but Athenian poets the perfecters."

49. See above, n. 22.

50. *Poet.* 4. 1448b25–34.

51. On what follows cf. Wilamowitz, "Die Textgeschichte der griechischen Lyriker," *Abhandl. Kön. Gesellsch. d. Wiss. Göttingen* N.F. 4, 3 (1901) 14–15.

52. Theophrastus, *On Poetic Art* (two works?), *On Comedy;* Dicaearchus, *The Life of Greece* (cultural history), *On Musical Contests* (including *On Dionysiac Contests*), *On Homer, On Alcaeus;* Aristoxenus, *On Melic Poetry, On Choruses, On Tragic Dancing, On Tragic Poets;* Demetrius of Phalerum, *On the Iliad, On the Odyssey, Homeric (Treatise)*; Heraclides Ponticus, *On the Date of Homer and Hesiod, On Archilochus and Homer, On the (Songs?) in Euripides and Sophocles, On the Three Tragic Poets, On Poetic Art and Poets, Homeric Solutions;* Phaenias of Eresus, *On Poets;* Praxiphanes, *On Poets* (?), (*On Poems*), *On Homer, On Hesiod* (?), *On Sophocles* (?); Chamaeleon, *On the Iliad, On the Odyssey, On Hesiod* (?), *On Alcman* (?), *On Sappho, On Stesichorus, On Lasos, On Pindar, On Simonides, On Anacreon, On Satyrs* (*i.e.,* on satyr-drama), *On Thespis, On Aeschylus, On Comedy;* Hieronymus of Rhodes, *On Poets.* In general see F. Wehrli, *Die Schule des Aristoteles,* Heft 10 (Basel-Stuttgart 1959) 121–125.

53. According to Diog. Laert. 2. 134; Suda s.v. Neophron; *hypothesis* Eur.

Medea. See Wilamowitz, *Hermes* 15 (1880) 487; F. Wehrli, *Die Schule des Aristoteles,* Dikaiarchos, 61–62.

54. The Academy took up the challenge. The pseudo-Platonic dialogue *Minos,* probably written in the late fourth century, asserts, rather nervously (321a): "Tragedy is an ancient thing hereabouts, not beginning with Thespis as people say, or Phrynichus; no, if you will just observe the evidence you will find it is a very ancient invention of this city."

55. See *A.'s Poet.* 110–112. A similar attempt was made to annex Homer: not indeed to claim that he was a Dorian, but that Dorians—in this case Lycurgus and Sparta—had been the first to value him and bring him to Greece. Reinhold Merkelbach, following in the footsteps of Wilamowitz, *Homerische Untersuchungen* (Berlin 1884) 271, shows, *Rhein. Mus.* 95 (1952) 32ff., that this belongs to a Dorian propaganda campaign aimed at overtopping Athens. The authorities cited for it, before Apollodorus, are Timaeus, Ephorus—and Aristotle quoted by Heraclides Ponticus!

56. *On the Proverbs of the Alexandrians,* chap. XXX; see *DTC* 105 and n. 18 above.

57. Above, p. 18.

58. Wilamowitz, *Einleitung* (see above, n. 6) 52–53: "wir sehen mit recht trauerspiel und lustspiel nur als zwei arten derselben gattung, der dramatischen poesie, an. darin sind uns die peripatetiker vorangegangen, und logisch ist es gewiss. nur hat es für Athen keinen sinn . . . komödie und tragödie zwei . . . grundverschiedene dichtungsgattungen . . ."

59. Schmid, *Gr. Lit.* II 82–83; Cantarella, *Eschilo* (Florence 1941) 67–69.

60. "Nothing to do with Dionysus"; but we need not accept the reversal from gay to grave which is presupposed by the ancient explanations of the saying. See Schmid, II 27–29, and below, p. 81.

61. See Pickard-Cambridge, *Dr. Fest.* 79–81.

62. See Else, "Origin" 31–32.

63. Reisch (see Introd., n. 6), p. 467; Else, "Origin" 31. Lesky suggests, *Trag. Dicht.* 22 n. 3, that *tragóidia* might have been formed directly on the model of *choróidia, palinóidia, prosóidia,* rather than from *tragóidos.* But the fifth-century evidence for these words is much too sparse (none for *palinóidia, choróidia; prosóidia* once each in Aeschylus and Critias) and oblique to serve as support. *Rhapsóidia* would be the obvious model; but that leads us back directly to *rhapsóidos (rhapsóidos: rhapsóidia : : tragóidos: tragóidia).* See also next note.

64. Thus *paróidos, paróidia,* denote a recitation by an individual; see F. Householder, *Class. Philol.* 39 (1944) 8, and Else, *A.'s Poet.* 84.

65. Lesky, *Trag. Dicht.* 11: "Im ersten Jahrzehnt unseres Jahrhunderts hebt sich in der Forschung, die um die Klärung des Tragödienursprunges rang, deutlich eine Periode des Sturmes und Dranges ab. Damals erscholl unter der Einwirkung von Folklore und Ethnologie der Kampfruf: Los von Aristoteles!"

66. The concept which was given wide currency by Frazer's *Golden Bough,* part III, "The Dying God."

67. K. Kerenyi, *Saeculum* 7 (1956) 385–394, especially 392; but cf. Jeanmaire, *Dionysos* (Paris 1951) 46–47.

68. See Introd., n. 2. Del Grande, TPAΓΩIΔIA (Naples 1952) 270–272, gives a most interesting analysis of the motives of Murray's theory, showing that it really grows out of the Christian liturgical year.

69. Even when tragedy has two actors (after 500), or three (after 463?), actual combats are never shown.

70. L. R. Farnell, *The Cults of the Greek States* (Oxford 1896–1909) V 234–237; and see *JHS* 29 (1909) xlvii.

71. (Sir) William Ridgeway, *The Origin of Tragedy* (Cambridge 1910), especially 47–50; cf. his *The Dramas and Dramatic Dances of Non-European Races* (Cambridge 1915).

72. A. Dieterich, "Die Entstehung der Tragödie," *Archiv für Religionswissenschaft* 11 (1908) 163–196.

73. "Der Ursprung der Tragödie," *Neue Jahrbücher für das klassische Altertum* 27 (1911) 609–642, 673–696 (reprinted in *Opuscula Selecta* I [Lund 1951] 61–145); see also his *Geschichte der griechischen Religion* (Handbuch d. Alt.-Wiss.), vol. I, ed. 2 (Munich 1955) 162, 234, 572.

74. I am happy to see that Professor Kitto now says·this in round terms: *Theatre Survey* 1 (1960) 1–17. —Note that I say "festival of the Greater Dionysia," not "cult of Dionysus."

75. *Trag. Dicht.* 15. Briefly we can say that *logos* here means 'rational discourse,' 'reason.'

76. A. Peretti, *Epirrema e tragedia* (Florence 1939) chap. IX, "La rhesis arcaica," 227–253.

77. See J. de Romilly, *La crainte et l'angoisse dans le théâtre d'Eschyle* (Paris 1958), and below, pp. 85, 89–90, 97.

78. See E. R. Dodd's ed. of Eur. *Bacchae,* Introd., pp. xxviii–xxxii, on Aeschylus' Dionysiac dramas.

79. Of the five titles of Thespian plays given in the Suda, only one (*Pentheus*) indicates a Bacchic subject; and the titles are very likely not genuine: see chap. III n. 2.

Chapter II. Solon and Pisistratus: The Attic Matrix

1. "Hero" is meant here in its ordinary sense, not the special Greek sense involved in the term "hero-cult."

2. W. F. Otto, in the volume of his collected addresses and essays entitled *Das Wort der Antike* (ed. K. von Fritz, Stuttgart 1962) pp. 163–167, gives a brilliant summary of the reasons for this.

3. The earliest extant discussion of Solon as a statesman is in Aristotle's *Constitution of the Athenians,* chaps. V–XI, with a rich sampling of Solon's own utterances (we owe most of the extant political fragments to Aristotle). For modern treatments see Ivan M. Linforth, *Solon the Athenian* (Berkeley, Calif., U. of C. Publs. in Class. Philol. 1919; includes text and translation of the fragments, with commentary); Kathleen Freeman, *The Life and Work*

of Solon (Cardiff 1926, with a translation); on Solon's agricultural and economic reforms, W. J. Woodhouse, *Solon the Liberator* (Oxford 1938).

4. Pictured, e.g., in Ernst Buschor, *Griechische Vasen* (Munich 1940) Plates 12, 15; George Karo, *An Attic Cemetery* (Philadelphia 1943) Plate 11; R. M. Cook, *Greek Painted Pottery* (Chicago 1960) Plates 4a, 5.

5. The most recent Greek text of Solon is in E. Diehl, *Anthologia Lyrica Graeca,* ed. 3, Fasc. 1 (Leipzig 1949) 20–47. The translations are my own. Several of the poems from which I quote, including the Prayer to the Muses, are translated by Richmond Lattimore in *Greek Lyrics,* ed. 2 (Chicago 1960) 18–23. The passages quoted here from the Prayer to the Muses are no. 1, lines 1–4 and 27–28, in Diehl; pp. 18–19 in Lattimore.

6. 3, 5–9 D(iehl); p. 20 L(attimore).

7. *Diallaktên kai archonta:* Aristotle, *Ath. Pol.* 5, 2.

8. Shield: 5, 5 D.; Wolf: 24, 26 D.; p. 22 L.

9. 5, 1–4 D.; p. 21 L.

10. 3, 32–39 D.; p. 21 L. Werner Jaeger devoted a famous essay to this poem: "Solons Eunomie," *Sitzungsber. Berlin Akad.* (1926) 19–85.

11. Schmid, *Gr. Lit.* II 23: the marks of the old Athenian character are "Konzentration auf das Ethisch-Politische, geringes Interesse für mechanische Erklärung der Naturvorgänge, Betonung des Verhältnisses zwischen Mensch und Gott, Suchen nach einer objektiven Instanz, einer unerschütterlichen Norm menschlichen Lebens . . . — nach 'Gerechtigkeit.' "

12. 24, 3–6 D.; p. 22 L.

13. Hesiod, *Theogony* 30–32. Pindar, another Boeotian, similarly tells in his own words (*Pythian* 8, 56–60; but another explanation is favored in E. Thummer, *Pindars Religiosität* [Comment. Aenip. XIII, Innsbruck 1957] 32) how the hero Alcmaeon met him on the road to Delphi and prophesied to him. On a different occasion, during a storm, Pindar saw a statue of the Great Mother walking toward him: *Schol. Pyth.* 3, 137b Drachmann. Toward the end of his life Demeter (*Vita Ambr.* p. 2, 6 Dr.) or Persephone (Pausanias 9, 23, 3) appeared to him in a dream, reproaching him for not having honored her in song. The details may not be reliable, but they are suggestive of a certain type of religiosity.

14. 17 D.

15. See Werner Jaeger, *The Theology of the Early Greek Philosophers* (Oxford 1947) 93–94 (on Parmenides); 112–113 (Heraclitus); 133, 143–144 (Empedocles).

16. The natural enough supposition of Welcker and others, prompted in part by Aristophanes, *Frogs* 886–887, that Aeschylus was a particular devotee of the Demeter of his native town, seems to be refuted by the story in Clement of Alexandria, *Stromateis* 2, 60, 3 (also, though without the clinching detail, in Aristotle, *Eth. Nic.* 2, 1111a10 and in the anonymous commentator on the passage, ed. Heylbut) that the poet, when prosecuted for revealing some of the secrets of the Eleusinian Mysteries, secured acquittal by proving that he was not even an initiate. On Aeschylus' freedom from cult or sectarian dogma see Schmid, *Gr. Lit.* II 185–186; Jaeger, *Paideia,* vol. I (Oxford 1939) 235–236.

17. Darius in the *Persians* is not a counter-instance. The ideas that he expounds include nothing that goes beyond the commonplaces about mortal pride and its punishment by the gods.

18. See below, p. 63.

19. See Jaeger, *Paideia* I 249–251.

20. Plutarch, *Solon* 25, 6ff.

21. See nos. 12–14; 20; 26 Diehl.

22. Schmid, *Gr. Lit.* I 356; Wilamowitz, *Einleitung in die griechische Tragödie* 69–70; H. Fränkel, *Dichtung und Philosophie des frühen Griechentums* (Lancaster, Pa. 1951) 207.

23. See Linforth, *Solon the Athenian* 41–45.

24. Plutarch, *Solon* 8; and see Else, "Origin" n. 62.

25. Cited with critique by Freeman, *The Life and Work of Solon* 169–172.

26. No. 2 D.

27. "Origin" p. 36.

28. 24, 1–8 and 25–27, D.; p. 22 L. Note how crisply the final simile, for all its un-Homeric brevity, brings home Solon's imperiled position and his heroic stance; for in the *Iliad* the lion or boar or wolf that turns and faces the dogs is an analogue of the hero. It is a Homeric image used un-Homerically: now the poet himself is the wolf.

29. 25, 6–9 D.

30. 23, 1–7 D.

31. On this subject see the excellent article by Frederic Will, "Solon's Consciousness of Himself," *TAPA* 89 (1958) 301–311. I am especially glad to find myself in agreement with Will because our treatments of Solon were written quite independently of each other.

32. Nos. 1 and 2 Diehl. One is reminded that Nietzsche chose Archilochus, of all Greek poets, to illustrate his paradox that the lyric poet, just when he seems most subjective and individualistic, is most objective and self-forgetting.

33. No. 67a Diehl.

34. See Bruno Snell, *The Discovery of the Mind* (Oxford 1953) chap. III, especially 51 (on Archilochus); 53 (on Sappho); 65.

35. Plutarch, *Solon* 29, tells a story which brings Thespis and Solon together: how Solon watched a performance of the new art of tragedy, with Thespis as actor, and took occasion to register emphatic disapproval of his "telling such great lies," i.e., impersonating somebody else. Similarly Diog. Laert. 1, 59. But such a remark would come with dubious grace from the author of "Salamis," and the story is so clearly Platonic in inspiration that its authenticity is suspect. See Else, "Origin" 39.

36. Arist. *Constitution of the Athenians,* chap. 14; Plut. *Solon* 30; Diog. Laert. 1, 49; see nos. 8–11 Diehl.

37. C. H. Whitman, *Homer and the Heroic Tradition* (Cambridge, Mass. 1958) 46–63; T. B. L. Webster, *From Mycenae to Homer* (London 1958) 158–186.

38. The Ram Jug: *Annual of the British School in Athens* 35 (1935) Plate 53; amphora: G. E. Mylonas, *Eleusis and the Eleusinian Mysteries* (Princeton

1961) Plate 29. Myths occasionally appear on other proto-Attic vases—for example, Heracles, Nessus, and Deianeira on an Attic stand found at the Argive Heraeum (*ca.* 660); Menelaus leading some warriors (but not from the *Iliad*) on another; by the Ram Jug Painter himself, Orestes about to kill Aegisthus and Clytemestra, and Peleus bringing the young Achilles to Chiron. In early black-figure, Heracles and Nessus again, and Perseus several times, with Gorgons and Harpies (Nessus Painter). Animals and half-animals—lions, centaurs, sphinxes, sirens, chimaeras, *gorgoneia*—are much more in evidence at this time (late 7th century) than heroes. Finally, Sophilus gives us the wedding of Peleus and Thetis and—at last—a horse race labeled "[funeral-]games of Patroclus." His contemporaries the KX and C Painters show the Judgment of Paris, Troilus pursued by Achilles, the birth of Athena, the death of Astyanax, the departure of Amphiaraus, Heracles entering Olympus. (The foregoing is summarized from J. D. Beazley, *The Development of Attic Black-Figure* [Berkeley 1951] 6–25.) Clearly, the chief interest of the time was not in myth, and when it is represented the source is anything and everything but our Homer. The centers of attention are Heracles, Perseus, the *antecedents* and *end* of the Trojan War, single combats (but almost never with the warriors named), sports events, and animals, animals, animals. Odysseus, if it is he, is brought on the scene by the ram; the "echo" of *Iliad* 23 is for the sake of the horse race. The focus varies, but it is never or almost never Homeric in the sense of literary influence from our *Iliad* or *Odyssey*.

39. By W. Zschietzschmann, *Jahrb. d. deut. archäol. Instituts* 46 (1931) 45–60. However, Z.'s suggestion was energetically denied by Andreas Rumpf, *Festschrift Poland* (*Philol. Wochenschr.* 52 [1932] no. 35/38) 281–283, and K. F. Johansen, *Iliaden i tidlig Graesk Kunst* (Copenhagen 1934) 132–134 n. 1.

40. Solon: Diog. Laert. 3, 57; Suda s.v. *hypobolé.* Hipparchus: [Pl.] *Hipparchus* 228b.

41. See G. W. Bolling, *Ilias Atheniensium* (Lancaster, Pa. 1950) 5–6; D. L. Page, *The Homeric Odyssey* (Oxford 1955) 73, 97, 135, 144; J. A. Davison, "Peisistratus and Homer," *TAPA* 86 (1955) 1–30.

42. G. S. Kirk, *The Songs of Homer* (Cambridge 1962) 97–98, 204–210, 340; Cantarella, *Eschilo,* 52–53.

43. All this notwithstanding Solon's famous aphorism (actually a proverb to which he gave wider currency), "The bards tell many lies."

44. See Farnell (referred to above, chap. I n. 70).

45. We do not know whether dithyrambic contests were included in the program of the Dionysia under the tyrants (see Pick.-Camb. *DTC* 23, 25, on Lasos) or only under the democracy after 510.

Chapter III. Thespis: The Creation of *Tragóidia*

1. *Wasps* 1479: "the ancient dances with which Thespis used to compete." For the old and vexed question whether this is our Thespis or another one,

a dancer by the same name, see Ervin Roos, *Die tragische Orchestik im Zerrbild der altattischen Komödie* (Lund 1951) pp. 107–115.

2. The Suda gives the names of four plays, *Games of Pelias* or *Phorbas, Priests, Young Heroes,* and *Pentheus.* But we have no idea where these titles came from. The plays they designate may be the ones, or some of the ones, which Aristoxenus accused Heraclides Ponticus of having fabricated and attributed to Thespis (Diog. Laert. 5, 92). See further *DTC* 117.

3. See Fick-Bechtel, *Die griech. Personennamen,* ed. 2 (Göttingen 1894); E. Locker, *Glotta* 22 (1934) 85–87 (short names in *-is*); E. Schwyzer, *Griech. Gram.* (Handbuch d. Alt.-wiss.) I 636–637. It should be added that the stem *thesp-* appears nowhere else in Attic names, except for a Thespios from the 2nd cent. B.C. (?): Kirchner, *Prosop. Att.* no. 7205. In other words Thespis seems to be an isolated formation among Attic names. —A headless herm found at Aquae Albulae near Rome in 1902 (*Notizie degli Scavi* 1902, p. 111) carries the inscription *Thespis Themônos Athênaios,* i.e., "Thespis, son of Themon, Athenian." Themon also is a *Kurzname.* But we have no idea where this information, if it is information, came from.

4. Both usages are found, the former especially in the epic. Astyanax was not "lord of the city" nor Telemachus a "far-fighter," but their fathers were. We know that the bardic profession often passed from father to son; cf. the Homeridae of Chios.

5. Obviously much depends on one's dating of Thespis and one's guess—it cannot be more—as to the exact chronological and spiritual relationship between his new *tragôidia* and the recitations at the Panathenaea. See further below.

6. *Stromateis* 1, 79.

7. Above, chap. I n. 18. Pickard-Cambridge, *DTC* 102–103, shows that a famous line from Eratosthenes' *Erigone* quoted by Hyginus, 2, 4: "At that time the Icarians danced around a goat," probably has nothing to do with tragedy.

8. Above, pp. 23–24.

9. See Wilamowitz, *Hermes* 21 (1886) 620 n. 2. M. Pohlenz, *Nachrichten Akad. Gött. Phil.-Hist. Kl.* (1928) 298–321, and E. Tièche, *Thespis* (Leipzig and Berlin 1935) 22 ff., attempt to show that in the attachment of Thespis to Icarios another and later theory was at work, Alexandrian rather than Peripatetic, which sought to derive tragedy from rustic revels (*trygôidia,* i.e., comedy) rather than satyr-play. But there are some difficulties about the distinction and I do not think the last word has been said on the subject.

10. According to tradition Icarios (-ia) was the place where Dionysus first landed in Attica, after his voyage across the Aegean, and thereafter a kind of Dionysiac headquarters for Attica (the modern name for the locality is Dionyso).

11. App. 3.

12. It may be asked why I am ready to accept this piece of evidence, brief and indirectly attested as it is, when I reject so much of what Aristotle says or appears to say in the *Poetics* as theorizing. The answer is twofold: (1) As

to its authenticity: Themistius is an excellent authority, learned, intelligent, and deeply versed in Aristotle's works. See Lesky, *Trag. Dicht.* 41. (2) As to its value as evidence: I do not believe that Aristotle had available to him any archives, or indeed any systematic written documents, from the period before the democratic reorganization of the tragic contests in 502/501 B.C. I am prepared to believe, however, that some general tradition of what Thespis had done survived into the fifth century and so eventually (for example, through Sophocles' book *On the Chorus,* mentioned by the Suda) reached Aristotle. And I am the more prepared to believe this because the quotation in Themistius has the appearance of representing a native Athenian tradition, uncontaminated by the Dorian propaganda claiming an origin out of satyr-drama, or even by Aristotle's own probable sympathy with the Dorian cause.

13. See n. 1 above.

14. *Einleitung in die gr. Trag.* 87–88.

15. Aurelio Peretti, *Epirrema e tragedia* (Florence 1939) 227–253.

16. See below, pp. 71–73.

17. "Origin" (see Bibliographical Note) 23–25.

18. Most convenient account, with the extant fragments, in Pickard-Cambridge, *Dr. Fest.* 103–126.

19. See Schmid, *Gr. Lit.* II 38 n. 5.

20. On the following see my article "ΥΠΟΚΡΙΤΗΣ," *Wiener Studien* 72 (1959) 75–107.

21. "The Case of the Third Actor," *TAPA* 76 (1945) 1–10.

22. Walter Nestle, *Die Struktur des Eingangs in der attischen Tragödie* (Stuttgart 1930) 13, 23.

23. *Epirrema e tragedia,* referred to above, n. 15.

24. Lesky, *Trag. Dicht.* 33–34.

25. The nearest thing to this was perhaps the recitation of verses of Archilochus, which we know to have taken place: Heraclitus fr. 42 Diels; Pl. *Ion* 531a; Clearchus in Athen. 14, 620c.

26. See the *index rerum* of *A.'s Poet.,* p. 663, s.v. 'Pathos.'

27. Suda s.v. Phrynichos.

28. *Eschilo* (Florence 1941) 41–42; see also Jaeger, *Paideia* I 239–241.

29. Yet does not the death of President Kennedy, and the profound emotional reaction to it around the world, prove that it is possible?

30. "Origin" 34ff.

31. *Eschilo* 92–96; cf. Lesky, *Trag. Dicht.* 15: "der logosbestimmten Welt der Tragödie." —For the same reason I cannot see any need to associate the tragic mask with Dionysus. See Pickard-Cambridge, *DTC* 110–112.

32. Peretti, *Epirrema e tragedia* (Florence 1939) 229–253; R. Hölzle, *Zum Aufbau der lyrischen Partien des Aischylos* (Marbach 1934); also E. Reiner, *Die rituelle Totenklage der Griechen* (Stuttgart-Berlin 1938).

33. Wilamowitz, *Griechische Verskunst* (Berlin 1921, repr. 1958) 208: "eo adducor, ut legitimos hos numeros in naeniis Atheniensium fuisse credam," and cf. 204, 206.

34. Above, p. 55.

35. Gudmund Björck, *Das Alpha Impurum und die Attische Kunstsprache* (Uppsala 1950) 214–222; and cf. 358–361 on the intrusion of *ē* (where we would expect the "Doric" *ā*) in tragic choruses. Björck's remarks are fundamental to the discussion which follows.

36. On Homericisms in tragedy see Otto Hoffmann–Albert Debrunner, *Geschichte der griechischen Sprache,* I, ed. 3 (Berlin 1953) 113–115; on Ionicisms, *ibid.* 115–117 and H. W. Smyth, *The Sound and Inflections of the Greek Dialects,* I, Ionic (Oxford 1894) 69–73.

37. The most recent independent sampling of the evidence appears to be by Vittore Pisani in *Enciclopedia Classica,* sec. II, *Lingua e letteratura,* vol. V, *Storia della lingua greca* (Torino, etc., 1960) chap. IV. Pisani says at the beginning, p. 80, that the Dorian origin of the choral part is obvious from its language, which is the "solita lingua poetica colorita di dorico," while the dialogue is substantially Attic. But on the very next page he notes that many Atticisms also invade the choral parts and says that here the Doricism, being limited to a few traits like *ā* for *ē* and *-ân* for *-ôn* in the genitive plural of 1st declension nouns, often seems [he adds, "especially in Euripides"] to be a disguise ("travestimento") of the "corpo ionico-attico che forma la sostanza dell' espressione." The discrepancy between the two statements is obvious. Pisani's examples fully bear out the second one, and not only for Euripides.

38. See G. S. Kirk, *The Songs of Homer* (Cambridge 1962) 192–196.

39. It is worth noting also that not a single major choral poet was a Dorian native of a purely Dorian city. Arion came from Aeolic Lesbos; Alcman was perhaps a Lydian, perhaps an Ionian; Stesichorus was a native of the linguistically mixed Himera, Ibycus of the equally mixed Rhegium; Pindar was a Boeotian; Simonides and Bacchylides were Ionians from Ceos.

40. Hoffmann-Debrunner, *Geschichte der griechischen Sprache,* 108–109.

41. On Lasos see Pickard-Cambridge, *DTC* 22–24. Lasos came from the "Dryopian" town of Hermione near the Argolid. Whether a Dorian or not, he undoubtedly followed the Dorian tradition in the dithyramb, and the Ionian Simonides surely did the same.

42. *DTC* 23.

43. On the other side, that of the over-all form, a converse influence is also possible, from tragedy to dithyramb. This has often been suggested for the curious "Theseus" (no. 18) of Bacchylides, which the Alexandrians apparently labeled a dithyramb. —We do not know what to make of the statements in the Suda, s. vv. Pindaros and Simonides, that these poets also wrote tragedies.

44. Nilsson, "Der Ursprung der Tragödie" (cited above, chap. I n. 73) 618–624.

45. Plut. *Solon* 21.

46. See above, chap. II n. 35, on Plutarch's account of their meeting.

47. It is not impossible that family pride also had something to do with it. Pisistratus was a Neleid, or claimed to be, and the glory of that family had certainly shone brighter in the heroic age than it had in Athens in his own time. Nestor is given a special place of honor in the *Iliad,* and he and his

son, Pisistratus' own namesake, are the first to welcome Telemachus on his journey in search of his father in the *Odyssey*. Pisistratus may have been well content to let the heroes of that greater time shine out above the luminaries of Attica (the ancestors of the Eupatridae) in the Homeric recitations and in tragedy.

Chapter IV. Aeschylus: The Creation of Tragic Drama

1. Between 499 and 496 B.C.: Suda s. vv. Choirilos and Pratinas.

2. Introduction of female masks: Suda; sweetness of his songs: Aristoph. *Wasps* 220, *Birds* 750; multifariousness of his dance movements: Plut. *Quaest. conviv.* 8. 732. See Lesky, *Trag. Dicht.* 46–48. So far as our evidence goes, Phrynichus' invention of "historical tragedy"—if he did invent it—came after the beginning of Aeschylus' career: *Capture of Miletus,* probably 492; *Phoenician Women,* probably 476. See below, p. 88.

3. See H. Bogner, "Kleisthenes und die Tragödie," *Historische Zeitschrift* 154 (1936) 1–16.

4. See above, p. 18.

5. Pick.-Camb. *Dr. Fest.* 74–79.

6. Lesky, *Gesch. d. griech. Lit.,* ed. 2 (Bern 1963) 259, suggests 515, in harmony with the marked increase in the number of representations of satyrs on vases after 520.

7. Diog. Laert. 2, 133; Pausanias 2, 13, 6, say that ancient critics gave Aeschylus first place in satyr-drama. See Thalia P. Howe, "The Style of Aeschylus as Satyr-Playwright," *Greece and Rome* 2nd ser. 6 (1959–1960) 150–165.

8. Athenaeus 8, 347c.

9. There are good remarks along these lines in H. J. Muller, *The Spirit of Tragedy* (New York 1956) 61, 70–77.

10. See Gilbert Murray's book mentioned above, p. 78, which gives an excellent *précis* of some of Aeschylus' great qualities as a poet and a dramatist.

11. See G. S. Kirk–J. R. Raven, *The Presocratic Philosophers* (Cambridge 1957) 117ff. ('justice' and 'injustice'), and note the last sentence on p. 142: "Incomplete and sometimes inconsistent as our sources are, they show that Anaximander's account of Nature, though among the earliest, was one of the broadest in scope and most imaginative of all"—a statement which, slightly recast, could equally serve to characterize Aeschylus among the tragedians. Similarly W. Jaeger, *The Theology of the Early Greek Philosophers* (Oxford 1947) 23.

12. One thinks of the brilliant title of Karl Reinhardt's brilliant book, *Aischylos als Regisseur und Theologe* (Bern 1949).

13. See above, p. 6.

14. For better or worse the *Prometheus* is passed over in what follows. I hope to deal with it at a later time, but must confess meanwhile that if the play is genuine (and doubts about its authenticity are not simply to be brushed away, as too many scholars have done in recent years; see Lesky's renewed

protest, *Gesch. d. gr. Lit.,* ed. 2, p. 284) I cannot understand it, either technically or ideologically, except as representing a complete break with the rest of Aeschylus' work—a break so violent, in fact, as to require a very special explanation.

15. The *Women of Aetna,* about whose structure we learn surprising things (four changes of scene in the same play?) from a scrap of a *didaskalia, Oxyrh. Pap.* XX no. 2257, fr. 1, belongs to our period: it was produced in 470.

16. It began sometime between 499 and 496; see n. 1 above.

17. See my article referred to above, chap. III n. 21. Use of the second actor by Phrynichus cannot be proved but is probable at least for his *Alcestis:* see the reconstruction by Lesky, *Sitzungsber. Vienna* 203 (1925) no. 2, pp. 63–64. Unfortunately the play cannot be dated.

18. See above, chap. III n. 20.

19. H. D. F. Kitto, *Greek Tragedy,* ed. 3 (London 1961) 32.

20. At this point my reading of the situation differs from Professor Kitto's. He (see previous note) takes Aeschylus' concentration upon a single hero to be a matter of his own choice or interest, whereas I regard it as inherent in the tragic form—Thespis' *tragóidia*—from the beginning. The heroic *pathos* is irremediably single.

21. See W. Jens, "Strukturgesetze der frühen griechischen Tragödie," *Studium Generale* 8 (1955) 246–253, especially 248.

22. Down to line 1004. It is now generally agreed that the last 170 lines of the play as we have it, 1005–1078, are a later addition inspired by Sophocles' *Antigone.*

23. See Lesky, "Göttliche und menschliche Motivierung im homerischen Epos," *Sitzungsber. Heidelberger Akad.* (1961) no. 4.

24. 1, 29–32 Diehl.

25. *Ag.* 160–166, 179–181.

26. See chap. III n. 21.

27. Jacqueline de Romilly, *La crainte et l'angoisse dens le théâtre d'Eschyle* (Paris 1958).

28. For the list see Schmid, *Gr. Lit.* II 188 n. 8.

Index